YALE STUDIES IN ENGLISH
ALBERT S. COOK, Editor
LVII

WORDSWORTH'S THEORY OF POETIC DICTION

WORDSWORTH'S THEORY OF POETIC DICTION

A STUDY OF THE HISTORICAL AND PERSONAL
BACKGROUND OF THE LYRICAL BALLADS

BY

MARJORIE L. BARSTOW GREENBIE

NEW YORK / RUSSELL & RUSSELL

1966

148835

FIRST PUBLISHED IN 1917
REISSUED, 1966, BY RUSSELL & RUSSELL
A DIVISION OF ATHENEUM HOUSE, INC.
L. C. CATALOG CARD NO: 65—18806

PRINTED IN THE UNITED STATES OF AMERICA

PREFACE

The following study was undertaken as a doctoral dissertation under the direction of Professor Albert S. Cook of Yale University. To Professor Cook I am especially indebted, not only for stimulating guidance in the field of the English language in general, but for a most minute and painstaking criticism of the proof. To Professor Lane Cooper of Cornell University I owe a debt less easy of definition. Although he has not read the manuscript of this book, and is not responsible for particular statements herein, the inspiration and the direction that I received from him in my reading of Wordsworth as an undergraduate at Cornell has been the most vital element in my study of the poet; if there is anything good in this work of mine, it is ultimately derived from him. I also wish to make grateful acknowledgment to Professor Charlton M. Lewis for criticism received from him in his course on nineteenth-century poets in the Graduate School of Yale University.

My indebtedness to books I have tried to indicate in the footnotes. But, like many other students of Wordsworth, I wish to record my especial appreciation of the *Early Life of William Wordsworth* by Professor Émile Legouis. Although, in many instances, I have been forced to disagree with the conclusions of M. Legouis, I feel that without the stimulating example of his beautiful work, this study would have been impossible. In acknowledging my special indebtedness to books, I wish to make grateful mention of the beautiful collection of Wordsworthiana in the possession of Mrs. Cynthia Morgan St. John of Ithaca, New York, which she generously placed at my disposal.

In citing quotations from the prose of Coleridge and the poetry of Wordsworth, I have tried to retain the original punctuation and spelling, because they represent the usage of the authors themselves. In most other cases it has seemed best to standardize the spelling and punctuation for the sake of greater clearness and smoothness of reading.

CONTENTS

	PAGE
INTRODUCTION	vii
CHAPTER 1. Poetic Diction in 'Our Elder Poets'	1
CHAPTER 2. Poetic Diction in 'Modern Times'	19
CHAPTER 3. Wordsworth's Poetic Development Previous to the Meeting with Coleridge	67
CHAPTER 4. Coleridge and His Circle	113
CHAPTER 5. Coleridge and Wordsworth	126
CHAPTER 6. The Lyrical Ballads	141
BIBLIOGRAPHY	183
INDEX	186

INTRODUCTION

To those who read the poetry of Wordsworth in the light of Matthew Arnold's criticism, with the enthusiasm of all good Wordsworthians, the poet is primarily a teacher, a philosopher, a pure soul with a message of healing for a feverish world. So, indeed, he regarded himself. 'I wish either to be considered as a teacher, or as nothing,'[1] he writes; and his wish has been fulfilled. But too often he is so considered to the exclusion of a proper interest in his merits as a stylist, as a great and peculiarly self-conscious artist 'in a kind absolutely unborrowed and his own.'

To the two most finely gifted critics of his own generation he presented himself in a quite different light. It was not Wordsworth's philosophy that primarily interested Coleridge and Lamb; it was his style. To his philosophy they were both more or less antagonistic. Coleridge objected to the 'misty, rather than mystic, confusion of God with the world'[2] in poems like Tintern Abbey, though at the same time he believed Wordsworth capable of writing the first genuine philosophical poem in English. Lamb was inclined to make merry over Wordsworth's devotion to stocks and stones, and other inanimate objects, and to celebrate the superior attractions of the London streets.[3] But both immediately gave full recognition and homage to Wordsworth's unique gift of imaginative expression— 'the original gift of spreading the tone, the *atmosphere,* and with it the depth and height of the ideal world around forms, incidents, and situations, of which, for the common view, custom had bedimmed all the lustre, had dried up the sparkle and the dew drops.'[4]

[1] *L. W. F.* 1. 331.
[2] *Biographia Epistolaris* 2. 195.
[3] *Letters of Charles Lamb* 1. 190-191.
[4] *B. L.* 1. 59.

This gift, they felt, expressed itself in a diction 'highly *individualized* and characteristic'[1]—a 'diction peculiarly his own, . . . a style which cannot be imitated, without its being at once recognised as originating in Mr. Wordsworth.'[2] This style both Coleridge and Lamb believed they could distinguish without hesitation, wherever they encountered it. 'That

> "Uncertain heaven received
> Into the bosom of the steady lake"

I should have recognised anywhere,' writes Coleridge,[3] 'and had I met these lines running wild in the deserts of Arabia, I should have instantly screamed out, "Wordsworth!"' Lamb seems to hold a similar opinion. In his characteristic remarks on the edition of 1815, in which he proceeds from poem to poem, commenting with the refined Epicurean enjoyment of a connoisseur in language on the lines and phrases that most please his taste, he continually implies that Wordsworth has a distinct and recognizable manner. ' "Laodamia" is a very original poem,' he writes. 'I mean original with reference to your own manner. You have nothing like it. I should have seen it in a strange place, and greatly admired it, but not suspected its derivation.'[4] Again, in speaking of the extracts from *An Evening Walk* and the *Descriptive Sketches* included in the volumes of 1815, he remarks[5]: 'All the rest of your poems are so much of a piece, they might have been written in the same week; these decidedly speak of an earlier period. They tell more of what you had been reading.'

[1] *B. L.* I. 77.
[2] *B. L.* I. 80.
[3] *Memoirs* I. 139.
[4] *Letters of Charles Lamb* I. 353.
[5] *Ibid.* I. 354.

INTRODUCTION

This highly individualized diction always tempted Coleridge's powers of analysis. Indeed he was first led to his speculation on the difference between imagination and fancy by his attempts to define the peculiar quality of Wordsworth's poetry, as distinguished from verse that might seem more brilliant or clever or obviously skilful.[1] This analysis he carries further in his famous criticism of Wordsworth's style, and theory of style, in the *Biographia Literaria*.[2] 'Would any but a poet—at least could any one without being conscious that he had expressed himself with noticeable vivacity—have described a bird singing loud by, "The thrush is *busy* in the wood," or have spoken of boys with a string of club-moss round their rusty hats, as the boys *"with their green coronal?"*—or have translated a beautiful May day into *"Both earth and sky keep jubilee"*? or have brought all the different marks and circumstances of a sea-loch before the mind, as the actions of a living and acting power? or have represented the reflection of the sky in the water, as *"That uncertain heaven received into the bosom of the steady lake?"* Even the grammatical construction is not unfrequently peculiar; as *"The wind, the tempest roaring high, the tumult of a tropic sky,* might well be dangerous food to *him, a youth* to whom was given etc." There is a peculiarity in the use of the ἀσυνάρτητον (that is the omission of the connective particle before the last of several words, or several sentences used grammatically as single words, all being in the same case and governing or being governed by the same verb) and not less in the 'construction of words by apposition (*"to him, a youth"*).'

But Coleridge's brilliant and suggestive analysis of the characteristic features of Wordsworth's style—the unique and imaginative metaphors, the rich and often curiously felicitous diction, and the peculiar grammatical structure—

[1] *B. L.* 1. 60.
[2] *B. L.* 2. 83-84.

is, after all, rather fragmentary. Every remark is a seed-thought which needs development. Moreover, there is something exasperating and even misleading in the attitude that he chose to assume to the theory of diction which lies at the basis of the *Lyrical Ballads*. Coleridge, rather than Wordsworth, had been responsible for the critical propaganda[1] which, as he says, was the real cause of Wordsworth's unpopularity.[2] The Preface that he does not understand was half a child of his own brain,[3] written by Wordsworth to please him, and superintended and corrected by him.[4] Forgetting all this, he proceeds to adopt the hesitating manner of a stranger to statements that partly originated in his own fertile brain, and fails to supply the one invaluable thing that he only could supply—a more detailed account of the thoughtful and eager dialogues that were behind Wordsworth's somewhat inadequate utterances in print. Hence, though this criticism by Coleridge is the necessary starting-point for any investigation of Wordsworth's theory and practice, he was far from saying the last word on the subject. Wordsworth had more reasons than wounded vanity for his dissatisfaction with the remarks of his former collaborator.

Despite the natural unwillingness of lesser men to enter into competition with Coleridge and Lamb, it is astonishing

[1] *L. W. F.* 3. 121, 152.

[2] *B. L.* 1. 50-53.

[3] 'Although Wordsworth's Preface is half a child of my own brain, and arose out of conversations so frequent that, with few exceptions, we could scarcely either of us, perhaps, positively say which first started any thought (I am speaking of the Preface as it stood in the second volume), yet I am far from going all lengths with Wordsworth.'—Letter to Southey, July 1802. (*Letters of Samuel Taylor Coleridge* 1. 386.) Coleridge speaks as if the first consciousness of this difference in opinion were felt in 1802.—*Letters* 1. 375.

[4] *An Account of the Wordsworth and Coleridge MSS. in the Possession of Mr. T. Norton Longman*, p. 19.

that this analysis of Wordsworth's theory of poetic diction as illustrated in his style, so ably begun by them in the poet's own lifetime, should not have been carried on more systematically by the many critics who have praised Wordsworth so well. We find, indeed, a considerable number of scattered observations and brief studies of Wordsworth's style which are highly illuminating. For instance R. H. Hutton's little paper on *Wordsworth's Two Styles* is really discriminating. So also are Principal Shairp's delicate appreciation of the style of *The White Doe of Rylstone*, and Bagehot's essay on *Pure, Ornate, and Grotesque Art*. The various remarks of Hutchinson and Dowden—the accomplished students of Wordsworth's text—in their editions of the whole or parts of his work are always valuable. Moreover, the definitive text of Wordsworth's complete poems in the Oxford edition, and the Concordance of Professor Lane Cooper, have furnished the indispensable basis for a more scientific study of Wordsworth's poetic diction; and Professor Émile Legouis has set a shining example in the detailed analysis of the *Early Poems* in *The Early Life of William Wordsworth*. But these more scholarly efforts, added to the brilliant comments of Wordsworth's innumerable critics from Aubrey de Vere to Professor Harper, have been insufficient to dispel the popular misconceptions inherited from the reviewers. Wordsworth's readers to-day have more sympathy for his 'philosophy' than the Monthly Reviewer of 1815, but they hold much the same opinions concerning his style, and have scarcely more foundation for them.

The principal reason for this neglect is that the world has never taken Wordsworth's so-called theory of poetic diction seriously. Having jumped to the conclusion that Wordsworth's practice was inconsistent with his principles, most of his readers have failed either to recognize the scholarly background of much that he has to say, or to perceive the real comprehensiveness of his complete ideal of expression. In point of fact, Wordsworth is not inconsistent. His most dignified and elaborate style is inconsistent only with a single clause of his definition of the proper language of poetry, when that is detached from its context and arbitrarily taken to represent the whole.

The notion that poetry in general should employ the language of the 'lower and middle classes of society' was never Wordsworth's ideal at any time. It is only his definition of an experiment[1] that he chose to try in thirteen out of the nineteen poems by him in the first edition of the *Lyrical Ballads;* and the famous Preface is little more than a somewhat unwilling and frankly inadequate attempt to explain this same experiment.[2] Wordsworth himself suggests that an exposition of the whole theory would involve a complete history of literature and a social psychology.[3] After modifying his original suggestion until the 'language of conversation in the lower and middle classes of society' became in 1800, 'a selection of the real language of men in a state of vivid sensation,' and after softening this, in 1802, by a further emphasis upon the selective power of the poet, Wordsworth finally merges his special ideal in a

---

[1] 'The majority of the following poems are to be considered as experiments.' Advertisement to *Lyrical Ballads,* 1798.

[2] 'I was still more unwilling to undertake the task [of writing a systematic defense of the theory upon which the *Lyrical Ballads* were written] because adequately to display the opinions, and fully to enforce the arguments would require a space wholly disproportionate to the nature of a preface. . . . I have therefore altogether declined to enter regularly upon this defense.'—Preface to the *Lyrical Ballads* of 1800.

[3] 'For to treat the subject with the clearness and coherence, of which I believe it susceptible, it would be necessary to give a full account of the present state of public taste in this country, and to determine how far this taste is healthy or depraved; which again could not be determined without pointing out in what manner language and the human mind act and react on each other, and without retracing the revolutions, not of literature alone, but likewise of society itself.'—*Ibid.*

INTRODUCTION xiii

general respect for the purity and integrity of the English language—a new and more vital interpretation of that correctness so cherished by the eighteenth century. In the first collected edition of his poems in 1815 (which included the *Lyrical Ballads* and the poems of 1807, with a few additions of later origin), he relegates his original preface to the Appendix as containing 'little of special application to the greater part, perhaps, of the collection.'[1] Why has Wordsworth's own strict limitation of his 'theory' to a few poems been so systematically ignored?

But if the theory, in its more limited form, was merely an explanation of a small group of poems, much more was meant by it than commonly meets the eye of the casual

[1] 'The observations prefixed to that portion of these volumes which was published many years ago, under the title of "Lyrical Ballads," have so little of special application to the greater part, perhaps, of the collection as subsequently enlarged and diversified, that they could not with any propriety stand as an introduction to it. Not deeming it, however, expedient to suppress that exposition, slight and imperfect as it is, of the feelings which had determined the choice of subjects, and the principles which had regulated the composition of those Pieces, I have transferred it to the end of the second volume, to be attended to, or not, at the pleasure of the reader.' In all the complete editions between 1815 and 1845 this formed the first paragraph of the Preface which was reprinted from the volumes of 1815, as an introduction to the continually increasing collection of Wordsworth's poems. When this preface was transferred to the Appendix in the edition of 1845, the paragraph just quoted was replaced by the following note: 'In the succeeding editions, when the collection was much enlarged and diversified, this Preface [the Preface to the *Lyrical Ballads*] was transferred to the end of the volumes, as having little of special application to the contents.' In the reprints of the Preface of 1815 by Grosart, Knight, George, and Nowell Smith, the last edition has naturally been followed; and for this reason the important introductory paragraph is known only to those who have access to an early edition. When the critical edition of Wordsworth's literary criticism, which, despite the efforts of Nowell Smith, is still a desideratum, shall appear, it is to be hoped that so important an utterance will be restored.

reader. It was not a single isolated utterance. It had the wide background of English poetry and criticism for two centuries, and the narrower background of some very earnest literary experiment and study on the part, not of Wordsworth alone, but of an entire group of writers who were publishing in that open-minded periodical, *The Monthly Magazine*. Chief among these were Coleridge and Lamb. Not till we realize what Coleridge brought with him from Lamb to those memorable conversations in which the *Lyrical Ballads* originated do we begin to understand what was behind the curt sentences of the Advertisement of 1798.

It is not in their casual appearances in print that the most vital critical reflections of Wordsworth and Coleridge are to be sought, but in that remarkable oral discussion, begun by them in their long walks among the Quantock Hills, and continued day after day and year after year, not only by them, but by a larger circle, which included at various times Lamb, Southey, De Quincey, Hazlitt, Scott, Landor, and others. 'I have never felt inclined to write criticism,' said Wordsworth, 'though I have talked and am daily talking a great deal.'[1] And the echoes of this talk are everywhere heard in the criticism of the period—in Scott's edition of Dryden, in De Quincey's distinction between the literature of knowledge and the literature of power, which was originally Wordsworth's, in Coleridge's lectures, and later in chance remarks by Sara Coleridge and Aubrey de Vere. In order to understand the true relation of Wordsworth's criticism to his poetic creation, and to the literature of the past, we must, in imagination, continually supply this background of vivid conversation. And the beginnings of this are to be sought in the development of Wordsworth and Coleridge, in relation to their respective circles of friends and critics, long before they ever met.

[1] *L. W. F.* 3. 152.

Moreover, the reproduction of this background is particularly necessary because of the somewhat uncompromising tone of Wordsworth's formal criticism. Though his ideals were not wholly original, his personality was. What he took from without he translated into terms of his own experience, and converted to the substance of a peculiar and powerful nature—a nature unusually sensitive, and yet inflexible even to crudeness and awkwardness. Hence, since he always speaks from his own position, and does not easily adapt himself to an audience, it is necessary for his audience to adapt itself to him, and to discover in each case what is behind his utterances.

This is what has been attempted in this study. Accepting the poet's own declaration that any one who cares to study the matter will see that his principles are in accordance with the best traditions of English literature, I have begun with a review of the theories of poetic diction in England before the time of Wordsworth. Then, in the light of this study, and of such scanty evidence as we possess, I have tried to reconstruct the processes of critical thought which were responsible for the experiment of the *Lyrical Ballads,* and to show exactly how this thought affected his style—his vocabulary, his syntax, and his rhetorical devices—then and afterwards. And this I have done in the belief that his criticism and his practice are mutually illustrative, and that both, even in their exaggerations and possible mistakes, are of supreme value for the art of English poetry.

CHAPTER I.

POETIC DICTION IN 'OUR ELDER POETS.'

A great poet must create or recreate, not only the taste by which he is enjoyed,[1] but the language in which he writes. Like all artists, he must inform a medium already developed by others with the new spirit and the new life within him, thereby renewing and modifying the outward form also. But, unlike other artists, he derives his medium from two sources—from the written words of poets, who have thoughtfully adapted it to the purposes of beauty and delight, and from the lips of his daily associates, who have made a swift and haphazard adaptation of it to the purposes of immediate utility. Between these two—the written and the oral tradition—the poet, 'singing a song in which all other human beings join with him,'[2] must make his own synthesis, so that the artist and the plowman may both hear the message, each in his own tongue.

Of this duty the inheritors of the fertile English tongue have never been wholly neglectful. But their efforts have been complicated by a certain individualism in the English character. The Englishman, whether poet or plowman, likes to speak as he chooses. Between the characteristic phraseology of bards who invented their own language, and a rich popular speech, fond of short cuts, and uncritically hospitable to new locutions, the plain and open path of a generally intelligible and beautiful poetic diction has not always been easy to find. Nevertheless, it was not for want of self-criticism, and the unremitting efforts of many

---

[1] A remark attributed by Wordsworth to Coleridge. It is quoted, in slightly different forms, in the famous letter to Lady Beaumont (May 21, 1807: *Wordsworth's Literary Criticism*, p. 47), and in the *Essay Supplementary to the Preface*.

[2] Preface to *Lyrical Ballads* (in a passage added to the original preface in 1802).

generations, that the typical English style seemed to Matthew Arnold wilful, barbarous, and violent. So it had seemed to the most delicate spirits of Elizabethan England, wistfully looking to polished Italy and ancient Rome, and to their own well of English undefiled in Chaucer, and in the light of those standards discovering in their contemporary style some want of measure and grace. So it had seemed to the poets of the eighteenth century, scorning the rich and various language into which this Elizabethan diction had flowered as a luxuriant wildwood growth, which it was their task to reduce to French correctness and elegance. So it had seemed to Wordsworth, in whose eyes the effort of a century had resulted only in a phraseology so gaudy and 'licentious,' so lacking in the naturalness and good sense which had been constantly preached, that the discovery of a standard of expression which would protect the reader from the caprice of the poet seemed a matter of immediate and paramount importance.[1]

The most powerful and original of all these efforts was that of Wordsworth; yet its originality consisted, not in the creation of a new ideal of poetic diction, but in the vitality with which he informed an old one. Wordsworth was not the first to seek his poetic diction in a selection of the real language of men, as opposed to a traditional literary dialect. Chaucer had done it before, and Chaucer's master, Dante; and the method of Chaucer had remained the accepted one in English poetry, consciously imitated by Spenser, and received by others from Chaucer's own source—the vernacular literatures of the Continent, especially the Italian and French. Indeed, the modern poetry of Europe, in every tongue, is the result of a choice similar to that of Wordsworth on the part of poets, when Latin was still the speech of the cultivated. In England a power-

[1] Cf. Bagehot, *Literary Studies* 2. 389: 'A dressy literature, an exaggerated literature, seem to be fated to us; these are our curses.'

ful literary impulse from abroad, like that received from Italy in the sixteenth century, or that from France in the seventeenth century, has resulted in a new emphasis on a 'selection of the real language' of Englishmen who were not too deeply learned, as the only possible basis of poetic expression. Not till the latter half of the eighteenth century did the ideal of a special vocabulary for poetry become widely prevalent in England through the powerful influence of Gray; and even then it was opposed by the precepts and example of Goldsmith, Cowper, and Burns.

Hence, when Wordsworth began his attack on the 'gaudiness and inane phraseology' of contemporary verse, with the statement that his practice was in accord with that of 'our elder writers, and those in modern times who have been the most successful in painting manners and passions,'[1] he was making a claim easily established by that survey of English poetry which he invited his readers to undertake. Since a review of this sort throws Wordsworth's own criticism into its proper perspective, and emphasizes the new and vital elements in it, it will be well to let it introduce an examination of his own theory and practice. In so doing we may have the advantage of a running comment by Wordsworth himself on the work of his predecessors, since one of the excellences of his remarks, as compared with those of many poets before him, was their better critical basis in a study and deliberate appraisal of English literature in the various stages of its development. There are not many men of importance in the poetic history of England concerning whom Wordsworth has not left some illuminating comment; and what he left unsaid was generally said by Coleridge, whose studies were sometimes the source, and sometimes the result, of the vital thinking of his less bookish friend. Accordingly, we may proceed to build upon the foundation which they have already laid for us.

[1] Advertisement to the *Lyrical Ballads* of 1798.

Wordsworth and Coleridge divided English literature after Chaucer into two great periods—the age of 'our elder poets,' and 'modern times,' or the periods before and after Dryden's conscious break with the traditions of the past. For more than a century it had been the custom to date all literary civilization from the reign of Charles II, and to speak of the few great, unforgotten poets who had the misfortune to write before that time, as the rude forefathers of English verse, pre-eminent for the mighty force of their natural genius, but sadly lacking in art. Chaucer, Spenser, Shakespeare, and even Milton, had all been condescendingly rewritten into 'our language as it is now refined.' As a late development from this peculiar habit of refining, there had arisen the conception of a special dialect for poetry—a collection of phrases too delicate for ordinary use, or for the expression of vulgar real emotions that had a substantial existence outside of books. Against all this self-complacent criticism, Wordsworth vigorously appealed to the historical facts. The ideal of a special diction, or of any refinement except that of pure natural feeling, was not the ideal of the great age of English poetry before Dryden, he said, nor did it correspond to the best practice of poets after him. Was he right in this contention?

1. *Chaucer and Spenser.*

Concerning the practice of Chaucer, 'the first finder of our fair language,' and Wordsworth's special model in respect to language, there can be no doubt. With the well-developed literary and courtly medium of French at his command, he had turned to the mongrel vernacular, the real language of his countrymen, and had found an adequate poetic diction in a selection from that. Following here the footing of Chaucer's feet, Spenser had labored to restore, 'as to their rightful heritage,' 'such good and natural English words as have been long time out of use and almost clean disherited.' To him, or to his apologist 'E. K.,'[1] it appeared shameful that his countrymen should have 'so base regard and bastard judgment' of their own 'natural speech which together with their nurse's milk they sucked,' that they would not labor to garnish and beautify it by a development of its native resources. Since such 'old and obsolete words' as Spenser employs were 'most used of country-folk,' the reform of the young poet of the *Shepherd's Calendar* had something in common with that of the young poet of the *Lyrical Ballads*. As Wordsworth's interest in the language of the middle and lower classes of society incidentally involved a return to the speech of 'our elder poets,' so Spenser's return to the language of the one glorious 'elder poet' incidentally involved an approximation to rustic dialect.[2]

2. *Classicists and Purists.*

But Spenser did not stand alone. The purification and enrichment of the English language constituted one of the burning questions of the day. Scholars, poets, university wits, churchmen, and travelers—all had their contribution to make, a contribution immediately subjected to the criticism of the others. Sir Humphrey Gilbert anticipated

[1] Epistle addressed to Gabriel Harvey prefixed to the *Shepherd's Calendar* by E. K. I assume that E. K. represents the opinions of Spenser himself, whoever the writer of this apology may be.

[2] Coleridge includes practically all the *Faerie Queene* in his list of the poetry which illustrates Wordsworth's ideal of a beautiful diction which is, at the same time, the language of conversation. 'Spite of the licentiousness with which Spenser occasionally compels the orthography of his words into a'subservience to his rhymes, the whole "Faery Queen" is an almost continued instance of this beauty'—i. e. the beauty of verse 'in which everything was expressed just as one would wish to talk, and yet all dignified, attractive, and interesting.'—*B. L.* 2. 71.

Dryden and Matthew Arnold in planning an English academy, for the purpose of developing the resources of the vulgar tongue.[1] Under the influence of similar efforts on the Continent, Englishmen began to consider the development of the national speech a patriotic duty. All flourishing states and politic commonwealths, remarks Gabriel Harvey,[2] have made the most of their own languages. Italy, Spain, and France have spared no efforts to exalt their own tongues over those of Greece and Rome; only the English are backward in this respect. And Ascham observes that when a nation ceases to care for its own speech, its strength and moral integrity decline. A rude and disorderly style is a sign of a rude and disorderly character.[3]

The desired improvement had been partly attained through the deliberate importation of words from other languages, especially Latin. In 1542, at a meeting of Convocation, Bishop Gardiner had presented a list of about a hundred Latin words which he wished either retained in their original form, in the proposed revision of the Great Bible, 'for their genuine and native meaning, and for the majesty of the matter in them contained,' or 'fitly Englished with the least alteration.'[4] Some of the proposed additions are such familiar words as contrite (*contritus*), idiot (*idiota*), baptize (*baptizare*), martyr, ceremony (*ceremonia*), etc. Equally familiar to a reader of to-day are many of the words 'new made . . . of a Latin or French word' employed by Sir Thomas Elyot in *The Governour*, where he takes great care to provide a gloss in the text itself by coupling with them words of the same mean-

---

[1] Moore, *Tudor-Stuart Views*, pp. 96, 168-169.
[2] Gregory Smith I. 123-124.
[3] *Ibid.* I. 6. Cf. *Timber*, ed. Schelling, p. 32.
[4] *Tudor-Stuart Views*, pp. 89-90. Moore quotes from Mombert, *English Versions of the Bible*, 1907, pp. 230-231.

ing already in good use—'animate or give courage,' 'good kind or lineage,' 'facile or easy,' 'gross and ponderous'—or by giving the definition—'metamorphosis, which is as much as to say the changing of man into other figure or form.'[1]

But this zeal for patching the language with borrowings from abroad, to which Spenser objected, was condemned by men of scholarly instinct and training, like Sir John Cheke, Roger Ascham, Gabriel Harvey, and Sir Philip Sidney, who strove to do for the literary English of the Renaissance what Wordsworth tried to do for the language of the eighteenth century—to purify it from the arbitrary conceits and curious inventions in which the Elizabethan mind rejoiced, and to make it correspond, as far as possible, to the actual spoken vernacular. 'Among all other lessons this should first be learned,' says Thomas Wilson in the *Arte of Rhetorique*,[2] 'that we never affect any strange ink-horn terms, but so speak as is commonly received; neither seeking to be over fine or yet living over careless, using our speech as most men do, and ordering our wits as the fewest have done.' This same idea reappears in the remark attributed by Ascham to his master Sir John Cheke. The excellence of the language of Cæsar and Cicero, said Sir John Cheke,[3] was due to the fact that they were 'daily orators amongst the common people and greatest counsellors in the Senate house, and therefore gave themselves to use such speech as the meanest should well understand and the wisest best allow, following carefully that good counsel of Aristotle, *loquendum ut multi, sapiendum ut pauci.*' The result of this Elizabethan ideal in the poetry of the next century was observed by Coleridge: 'In the elder poets, from Donne to Cowley, we find the most fantastic, out-of-the-way thoughts, but in the most pure and genuine

[1] *Tudor-Stuart Views*, pp. 82-89.
[2] *Arte of Rhetorique*, ed. Mair, p. 162.
[3] Gregory Smith I. 40.

mother English; in the modern poets the most obvious thoughts in language the most fantastic and arbitrary.'[1]

The ideal of *loquendum ut multi* was applied to verse as well as to prose. Nothing was more sacred to the scholarly critics of verse in the sixteenth century, who were preparing the way for the marvelous flowering of the English genius in Shakespeare and his brother poets, than the idiom of the vernacular—those characteristic turns of speech which own no law but the habit of the people, what a Wordsworth of that day might have meant by 'language actually used by men.' 'Eschew strange words,' says Gascoigne,[2] 'or *obsoleta et inusita,* unless the theme do give just occasion. . . . You shall do very well to use your verse after the English phrase, and not after the manner of other languages. . . . Even as I have advised you to place all words in their natural and most common or usual pronunciation, so I would wish to frame all sentences in their mother phrase and proper *idioma.* Similarly Harvey objects to Spenser's altering the quantity of any one syllable otherwise than as 'our common speech and general received custom' will bear him out. 'We are not to go a little farther . . . than we are licensed and authorized by the ordinary use, and custom, and propriety, and idiom, and, as it were, the majesty of our speech, which I account the only infallible and sovereign Rule of all Rules,' he says, referring Spenser to Horace's *penes usum,* and *ius,* and *norma loquendi.*[3] This philosophy was expressed in more violent terms in the famous controversy between Nash and Harvey, in which each sent his opponent a list of his offenses against the sacred 'majesty of our

---

[1] *B. L.* I. 15. Cf. Schopenhaur, 'A poet should think like a genius, but talk the same language as any one else'—a saying used by A. J. George to illustrate Wordsworth's ideal of expression. See *Wordsworth's Prefaces,* pp. 105-106.

[2] Gregory Smith I. 52-53.

[3] *Ibid.* I. 117-119.

speech,' and loudly accused him of being that most
detestable of all literary criminals—an inkhornist.[1]

Nevertheless, these defenders of the idiom are the classicists of the day, opposing to every innovation not only
the law of their own language, but the shining examples
of antiquity. Yet theirs is a vital and wholesome classicism,
which looks, not to the letter, but to the spirit, of the law,
and really succeeds in translating the advice of Cicero,
Horace, and Quintilian into terms of their own needs
and experience. What could be more sensible than
Ascham's remarks on the style of the Latin classics? He
reminds his countrymen that the excellence of Cicero's
language was not something peculiar to himself—a literary
achievement; it was the reflection of the conversation of
the cultivated men of his time. The style of Cicero's letters, he observes, differs very little from the style of those
who wrote to him. Behind the eloquence of Cicero, and
the chaste and simple diction of Terence, lies a good habit
of daily speech, 'the pure fine talk of Rome, which was
used by the flower of the worthiest nobility that ever Rome
bred.'[2] Sir Philip Sidney represents the same classical
good sense, before it had become so rigid and self-complacent that it had ceased to be sensible at all. It leads
him, not only into a mild objection to Spenser's archaisms,
but to an anticipation of two of the leading principles of
Wordsworth's criticism. Quite in the spirit of the Appendix on Poetic Diction, he censures imitators of the classics
for reproducing the peculiarities which, in Cicero, are the
natural expression of genuine passion, when there is no
passion to be expressed. And so, he says, 'they do that
artificially which we see men do in choler naturally.'[3] Had

[1] *Ibid.* 2. 275.
[2] Gregory Smith 1. 28.
[3] *Ibid.* 1. 202. Cf. Wordsworth: 'The earliest poets of all nations generally wrote from passion excited by real events; they wrote naturally, and as men: feeling powerfully as they did, their language was daring and figurative. In later times, Poets,

critics and poets always retained this vivid consciousness that the classical writers were men like themselves, speaking 'naturally and as men,' instead of dead models of a perfect excellence, the utterances of Wordsworth would have been less necessary, and would have seemed less revolutionary. Again, Sidney anticipates Wordsworth in his method of testing verse by writing it into prose. Besides Chaucer's *Troilus*, the *Mirror of Magistrates*, and the *Shepherd's Calendar*, he remembered few verses that had poetical sinews in them; 'for proof whereof,' he says, 'let but most of the verses be put in prose, and then ask the meaning; and it will be found that one verse did but beget another, without ordering at the first what should be at the last; which becomes a confused mass of words with a tingling sound of rime, barely accompanied with reason.'[1]

However, we cannot say that the two doctrines especially associated with the name of Wordsworth appear in Elizabethan literary criticism in quite the form in which they are generally understood by his readers. The 'common use' or 'common speech' so often referred to is not strictly the language of conversation in the lower and middle classes. Though Wilson seems to object to the formation of a literary language, as opposed to the language of country-folk,[2] and Spenser implies that the well of English undefiled may be sought, in some instances, among the peasantry, Puttenham's definition of standard English—a selection of the real language of well-bred men within a radius of sixty miles around London[3]—seems to be the

and Men ambitious of the fame of Poets, perceiving the influence of such language, and desirous of producing the same effect without being animated by the same passion, set themselves to a mechanical adoption of these figures of speech, and made use of them, sometimes with propriety, but much more frequently applied them to feelings and thoughts with which they had no natural connexion whatsoever.'—Appendix to *Lyrical Ballads* of 1802.

[1] Gregory Smith 1. 196.
[2] *Arte of Rhetorique*, p. 164.
[3] Gregory Smith 2. 150.

accepted one. But these well-bred men are not pedants or university wits. They are men of affairs who speak clearly and intelligently, with more regard for matter than for words. Hence what Wordsworth perhaps was really seeking—a speech which was universally intelligible, and not the arbitrary creation of poets—was also the goal of these stout defenders of the 'common use' and the 'generally received custom.'

Again, though Dr. Johnson[1] says that before Dryden there was no poetical diction, no system of words especially refined and appropriated to poetry, it is generally implied in Elizabethan criticism that there is some difference, apart from metre, between the language of prose and the language of verse. Verse, says Puttenham,[2] is 'a manner of utterance more eloquent and rhetorical than the ordinary prose which we use in our daily talk, because it is decked and set out with all manner of fresh colors and figures, which maketh that it sooner inveigleth the judgement of men, and carrieth their opinion this way and that, whithersoever the heart by the impression of the ear shall be most affectionately bent and directed.' Nevertheless, though as much difference as this definition suggests is generally taken for granted, the efforts to purify the literary language are apparently directed toward prose and verse alike, and the same standard is usually applied to both.[3] This standard is to be found both in Horace's *Art of Poetry,* and in Cicero's *Orator* and Quintilian's *Institutes of Oratory.* The transference to verse of the ideal of a pure and universally intelligible diction which the greatest of Roman

---

[1] *Dryden* (*Lives,* ed. Hill, 1. 420).

[2] Gregory Smith 2. 8-9.

[3] Gascoigne says: 'You may use the same figures or tropes in verse which are used in prose.'—Gregory Smith 1. 52.

[4] The references to these authorities in Elizabethan criticism are too numerous to reproduce here. They may be found by consulting the excellent index at the end of the second volume of *Elizabethan Critical Essays.*

orators had acquired from a study of the Greek classics, on the one hand, and from his own experience as a 'daily orator among the common people,' on the other hand, tended to maintain a wholesome relation between poetry and prose.

The peculiar vitality of the Elizabethan classicism, crude as it was—this sense of a living contact of man with man in discipleship—enabled the critics of the age to approach more nearly to the spirit of their teachers than did many who felt themselves better instructed. Their faith in the necessity of preserving the native idiom at all costs, and of modifying the method of the Latin writers to serve their own purpose, nearly resembled the attitude of their masters to Greek—the attitude of Cicero, especially. He had always emphasized the necessity of following the law of his own language, inferior as it was by nature, and of admitting no foreign splendor incompatible with it. Those who had learned this lesson from him had learned something far better than a servile regard for correctness, and the disposition, not wholly unknown in antiquity, to plunder the classics of every figure of speech and every flower of poesy, and deck out their own verse in the unnatural spoils. This vital relation to Greek, and especially to Latin, poetry and literary criticism also enabled the Elizabethan critics to reproduce without too much exaggeration the classical attitude to verse and prose. This had more and more tended to emphasize the essential community between the two types of expression, without, however, failing to recognize the differences resulting sometimes from a difference in purpose, and always from a difference in the associations and the external effect of the medium. Thus the relation of the more scholarly Elizabethans to their ancient models was somewhat like the relation of Sidney's ideal poet to Nature. Lifted in the glory of their own freedom, they were preparing themselves to go hand in hand with the classics, not bound within the narrow warranty of their masters' gifts, but freely ranging only within the zodiac of their own wit.

3. *The Heirs of the Elizabethan Tradition in the Seventeenth Century.*

In the seventeenth century this wholesome Elizabethan tradition comes to a rather violent end—not to be revived again until the days of Coleridge and Wordsworth; and what Coleridge calls the second period of our language begins with the criticism and poetry of Dryden. During the earlier part of the century the Elizabethan ideals were maintained, not only by the plain and manly classicism of Ben Jonson, whom Dryden regarded as his master, but by two lesser poets, Drayton and Daniel, who made a peculiar appeal to Wordsworth and Coleridge, and were consciously imitated by them. Ben Jonson was apparently less attractive to the poets of the *Lyrical Ballads,* because he lacked the tenderness of heart that was associated with Wordsworth's ideal of simple expression; but he, too, battled bravely with the besetting sins of English style, and sought, in his own incomparable phrase, to 'redeem arts from their rough and braky seats, where they lay hid and overgrown with thorns, to a pure, open, and flowery light, where they may take the eye and be taken by the hand.'[1] But in this effort he did not strive to lift the literary language too far above the understanding of the vulgar multitude, whom, nevertheless, he frankly scorned. 'Pure and neat language I love,' he says, 'but plain and customary.'[2] This plain and customary style, which resulted from the striving after the golden mean in speech as well as in the rule of life, in Jonson's own time did not wholly escape the censure directed against simplicity in Wordsworth's day. 'The true artificer will not run away from

[1] *Timber,* ed. Schelling, p. 7.
[2] *Ibid.,* p. 59.

Nature as if he were afraid of her,' he observes, 'or depart from life and the likeness of truth, but speak to the capacity of his hearers. And though his language differ from the vulgar somewhat, it shall not fly from all humanity, with the Tamerlanes and the Tamer-chams of the late age, which had nothing in them but the scenical strutting and vociferation to warrant them to the ignorant gapers. . . . In the meantime, perhaps, he is called barren, dull, lean, a poor writer, or by what contumelious word can come in their cheeks, by these men who without labor, judgment, knowledge, or almost sense, are received or preferred before him. He gratulates them and their fortune. Another age or juster men will acknowledge the virtues of his studies.'[1] This suggests the very tone of Wordsworth with reference to the more popular and showy graces of Scott and Byron. Jonson's scorn of rhetoric 'that cannot suffer the sun or a shower, nor bear the open air,' his liking for 'strength and sinews' in verse or prose, echo Sidney, and anticipate the emphasis of Wordsworth and Coleridge on poetic substance—that substratum of fact and sense in verse which remains when it is turned into prose, or subjected to the test of intellectual analysis.

Meanwhile Drayton, too, was looking back with some complacency to the passing of the violent splendors of the 'Tamerlanes and Tamer-chams of the late age,' and the banishing of superfluous alliteration, forced antitheses, and far-fetched similitudes from a ridiculous natural history, which Euphues had made popular, and Sir Philip Sidney had striven to laugh out of existence. Sidney, writes Drayton,[2]

> throughly pac'd our language, as to show
> That plenteous English hand in hand might go
> With Greek and Latin, and did first reduce
> Our tongue from Lillie's writing then in use.

[1] *Timber,* ed. Schelling, pp. 26-27.
[2] Spingarn I. 137.

By its effect upon Wordsworth, Drayton's own energetic and manly, though not highly poetic, style, illustrative of the purified Elizabethan diction, furnishes another link between the ideals of this age and those of the reformation at the beginning of the nineteenth century. A still greater favorite with Wordsworth was Samuel Daniel, who, as Drayton said, wrote pure and excellent English, though his 'manner better fitted prose.' In Wordsworth's eyes this reputation for a diction too unadorned was naturally no discredit. Both in his literary criticism and in his own poetry, Daniel represented the native tradition, in opposition to those who had too fond a regard for alien elegancies. The ideal which Harvey, Spenser, and Sidney had applied to language, while they rather inconsistently dallied with classical metres, Daniel, in his controversy with Campion, applied to versification also. Every tongue, he says, has not only its own idiom, but its own peculiar music, endeared to the hearts of the people through long association. If we speak the language of our own people, why should we not sing the tunes of our people too? Let us keep our 'tinkerly sound' of rhyme despite the Greeks and the Romans, and cease this attempt to tune our ears to foreign harmonies.[1] In substituting the simple melody of the old popular ballads, and all the varied rhythms in which lyrical emotion naturally expresses itself, for the regular music of the heroic couplet, Wordsworth had worked in the spirit of this creed, though his objection to Pope's versification was only a corollary to his main thesis.

Meanwhile, the eternal adversary of pure English style, having been partly conquered in the form of Euphuism, reappeared in a new shape in the metaphysical poets, and left lingering traces of itself in the quaint and balanced prose of Sir Thomas Browne and his school. The fault of the metaphysical poets was not that they did not speak genuine English, but that they did not speak the

[1] Gregory Smith 2. 356-384.

'genuine language of passion.'[1] Nevertheless, in their pursuit of far-fetched similes and out-of-way thoughts, they displayed an intellectual power and a clearness of conception which kept Wordsworth and Coleridge from a wholesale condemnation of them. 'Read all Cowley; he is very valuable to a collector of English sound sense,' said Wordsworth, who nevertheless condemned the taste of an age in which the booksellers' stalls in London swarmed with the folios of this 'able writer and amiable man', while Milton was neglected.[2] But in Cowley's own age the metaphysical school did not escape the censure that always awaits offenders against Nature and simplicity, popular as they too often are. The rough versification of Donne, of whom Ben Jonson said that 'for not keeping the accent he deserved hanging,'[3] the wild metres of Cowley's Pindaric odes, and what Addison called the general Gothicism of taste among these curious thinkers, began to weary the gay spirits of the Restoration; and they turned with relief to the easy and mellifluous couplets of Waller, which demanded no effort on the part of the reader either to scan them or to comprehend their meaning. Thence came that mighty reform which in a single generation rendered the style of all English poetry hitherto hopelessly antiquated, and in 1675, the year after Milton's death, had produced an almost complete silence of all singers 'beyond the verge of the present age.'[4]

4. *Milton.*

But before we consider this new school of poetry and poetic diction, which prevailed down to the time of Wordsworth, and against which his criticism was chiefly directed,

[1] *B. L.* 1. 15.
[2] *Essay Supplementary to the Preface.*
[3] Spingarn 1. 211.
[4] *Ibid.* 2. 263.

we must turn aside for a moment to do honor to the splendid and lonely figure of Milton. It is not inappropriate that this brief mention of him should seem like a digression, an interruption of the main course of the discussion. Despite his manifold relations to literature and the political life of his own time, he seems to stand apart— to represent ideals which are peculiarly his own, and not, as in the case of Spenser and Shakespeare, simply the most glorious expression of a spirit common to a whole literary group. But this appearance of loneliness is due to the fact that Milton's proper background is not England alone, but the Continent. In spite of his intense patriotism, he thinks of himself as one of a European commonwealth of scholars and poets. As such he is not only an Englishman, but a representative of England. When we place him where he consciously belonged, in the main stream of the European Renaissance, we discover that he too is expressing, in terms of his continental relationships, the ideal which we have discovered in the most fruitful Elizabethan criticism, as well as in the prefaces of Wordsworth. Like his Italian masters, he thinks of the cultivated and literary language at his command as being, not a certain kind of English, but Latin; and the speech of the people as being, not the language of the country as opposed to that of the town, or the language of unaffected, well-bred men as opposed to the language of wits or pedants, but the whole of the English language as compared with the universal literary medium of Europe. When the choice between this literary language and the spoken vernacular is thus presented to his mind, he unhesitatingly elects the latter. 'I applied myself to that resolution which Ariosto followed against the persuasion of Bembo,' he says,[1] 'to fix all the industry and art I could unite to the adorning of my native tongue; not to make verbal curiosities the end (that were a toilsome vanity); but to be an interpreter and relater of

[1] Spingarn 1. 195.

the best and sagest things among mine own citizens throughout this island in the mother dialect. That what the greatest and choicest wits of Athens, Rome, or modern Italy, and those Hebrews of old, did for their country, I, in my proportion, with this over and above of being a Christian, might do for mine; not caring to be once named abroad, though perhaps I could attain to that, but content with these British islands as my world.' This sentiment was read and echoed by Wordsworth, who consciously tried to take up the work of Milton, and to carry out some of his plans for relating the best and sagest things among his own citizens.[1] Hence, even Milton, whose diction is the very antithesis of the 'language of conversation in the lower and middle classes,' and who certainly was responsible for some of the *dulcia vitia* in the poetry of the eighteenth century, proves upon examination to hold an ideal not altogether different from that of Wordsworth. The difference in their application of it was due to the immense range of Milton's historical and geographical imagination, and to his cosmopolitan culture. What a little group of lakes and hills was to Wordsworth, 'these British islands' were to Milton. He could localize his conceptions no further. As Wordsworth modifies the language of conversation in order to give it the melody and grace of the English poets whom he loves, so Milton raises and harmonizes the homely or over-luxuriant vernacular to the dignity of Greek and Latin.

[1] See *Prelude* 1. 168-169, and the brief preface to *Artegal and Elidure*.

CHAPTER 2.

POETIC DICTION IN 'MODERN TIMES.'

Milton was the last of the elder poets. Even in his own lifetime, a reform had begun which was to render him almost as obsolete as Spenser and Shakespeare. Despite the efforts of the Elizabethan classicists and purists, English poetry hitherto had never attained to that even simplicity which had been the ideal of many. There were still 'rough and braky seats' between its purple patches of flowery bloom. In Shakespeare there is no such relation between taste and genius, inspiration and moderating good sense, the glowing inner life and the gracious external manner, as that which we find in the tragedies of Sophocles; even in Milton there is an occcasional harshness and irregularity of style which seems crude beside the bright and limpid verse of Homer.[1] As the first flush of the wonderful creative energy of the Renaissance died away, this disproportion became more and more evident.[2] It was

---

[1] From the standpoint of the new school of poetic diction, Phillips, Milton's nephew, refers to 'Spenser, with all his rusty, obsolete words' and his 'rough hewn, clouterly verses,' and Shakespeare 'with all his unfiled expressions' and his 'rambling and indigested fancies' (Spingarn 2. 271). Dryden speaks in a similar tone, though in somewhat less picturesque terms: 'Yet it must be allowed to the present age that the tongue in general is so much refined since Shakespeare's time that many of his words, and more of his phrases, are scarce intelligible. And, of those which we understand, some are ungrammatical, others coarse, and his whole style is so pestered with figurative expressions that it is as affected as it is obscure' (Ker 1. 203).

[2] Sprat's analysis of the influence of the Civil Wars upon the language is interesting in this connection: 'The truth is, it has hitherto been a little too carelessly handled, and, I think, has had less labor spent about its polishing than it deserves. Till the time of King Henry the Eighth, there was scarce any man regarded it but Chaucer, and nothing was written in it which one would be

then discovered that, while poets had been singing so sweetly, and speaking so clearly and well, the laws of English prosody and grammar had never been really defined.[1] Each man had found them out for himself. The treatises of Gascoigne and Puttenham had been individual

willing to read twice but some of his poetry. But then it began to raise itself a little, and to sound tolerably well. From that age down to our late Civil Wars, it was still fashioning and beautifying itself. In the wars themselves (which is a time wherein all languages use, if ever, to increase by extraordinary degrees, for in such busy and active times there arise more new thoughts of men which must be signified and varied by new expressions), then, I say, it received many fantastical terms, which were introduced by our religious sects, and many outlandish phrases, which several writers and translators in that great hurry brought in and made free as they pleased, and withal it was enlarged by many sound and necessary forms and idioms. . . . And now, when men's minds are somewhat settled and their passions allayed, . . . if some sober and judicious men would take the whole mass of our language into their hands as they find it, and would set a mark on the ill words, correct those which are to be retained, admit and establish the good, and make some emendations in the accent and grammar, I dare pronounce that our speech would quickly arrive at as much plenty as it is capable to receive, and at the greatest smoothness which its derivation from the rough German will allow it.'—Spingarn 2. 113-14.

[1] See William Wotton's review of English grammar down to 1694 (Spingarn 3. 224-225). He says very sensibly: 'For, in the first place, it ought to be considered that every tongue has its own peculiar form as well as its proper words, not communicable to, nor to be regulated by the analogy of another language; wherefore he is the best grammarian who is the perfectest master of the analogy of the language which he is about, and gives the truest rules by which another man may learn it. Next, to apply this to our own tongue, it may certainly be affirmed that the grammar of English is so far our own that skill in the learned languages is not necessary to comprehend it. Ben Jonson was the first man that I know of that did anything considerable in it; but Lyly's grammar was his pattern, and for want of reflecting upon the grounds of a language which he understood as well as any man of his age, he drew it by violence to a dead language that was of a different make, and so left his work imperfect.' Some years before this (in 1679) Dryden had written: 'In the age of that poet [Æschylus] the

efforts only; there had been no general and consistent attempt on the part of the whole literary world to discover exactly what constituted the virtues and vices of poetic style. If the classical and puristic criticism, which had hitherto been the organizing and restraining influence in English verse, was not to fail entirely, it must cease to be general and spasmodic. It was now necessary to descend to minutiæ, and to develop a standard so narrow and definite that its demands should be always quite unmistakable. It was not enough to say that poets should make a judicious selection from the spoken language. All the literary expressions that did not occur in that language must be interdicted one by one, specifically and by name; and the interpretation of the phrase, 'judicious selection', must not be left to the judgment of every scribbler. The wild individualism of the metaphysical school had shown that private judgments were not to be trusted.

Hence came the reform of Dryden and his school. They did not invent a new standard; they merely tried to make the Latin standard inherited from Sidney through Ben Jonson as specific and practical as possible. It was the old war, conducted with slightly different tactics, on the old enemy in a new guise, with substantial re-enforcements from France. Even before the Revolution the sons of Ben, with their doughty sire, had begun to anticipate the conception of a more chastened style and a smoother versification.[1] Ben Jonson seemed to Dryden to illustrate the

Greek language was arrived to its full perfection; they had amongst them an exact standard of writing and speaking. The English language is not capable of such certainty; and we are so far from it that we are wanting in the very foundation of it, a perfect grammar' (Preface to *Troilus and Cressida*, Ker 1. 203). In 1693 he wrote: 'We have yet no English *prosodia*, not so much as a tolerable dictionary, or a grammar; so that our language is in a manner barbarous' (*ibid.* 2. 110).

[1] See Schelling, 'Ben Jonson and the Classical School,' *Pub. Mod. Lang. Assoc.* 13. 235.

ideal of correctness which was to dominate the eighteenth century. Jonson, he said, 'is to be admired for many excellencies; and can be taxed with fewer failings than any English poet.'[1] But to the Horatian criticism of the royal Ben was now added the Horatian criticism of Malherbe and Boileau and the new French Academy,[2] which insisted on the need of discarding the tawdry and outworn decorations of the old poetic diction, in favor of a judicious selection from the spoken language. In England, as in France, 'an attack was directed against distortions and intricacies in all forms of literature. The substitution of general for technical terms and imagery, the elimination of the Latin coinage of Browne and his school, . . . the attempt to make literature approximate more and more to conversation, the trend toward precision of word and idea—these are different phases of the same movement, and all find reasoned expression in the criticism of the period.'[3] A certain sobriety and externality in the new criticism was mainly due to the loss of energy which had made the reform necessary and possible. The splendor and bravery of the old lawlessness was gone, and with it some of the freedom and spirit which had animated the stout defenders of the law. But the vivid animation was no longer necessary. Henceforth there was to be a steady and peaceable conquest.

The relation of the criticism of Dryden and Pope to the age of Shakespeare and the aberrations of the metaphysical school may be best described in the language of Petit de Julleville concerning the relation of Malherbe and Boileau

[1] Ker 1. 138. Dryden notes also that Jonson 'did a little too much Romanize our tongue.'—*Ibid.* 1. 82.

[2] 'La principale fonction de l'Académie sera de travailler avec tout le soin et toute la diligence possible, à donner des règles certaines à notre langue, et à la rendre pure, éloquente et capable de traiter les arts et les sciences.'—Quoted by Petit de Julleville from the statutes of the Academy, *Histoire* 4. 138.

[3] Spingarn, p. xlviii.

to the poetry of the Pléiade. The situation is almost exactly parallel. 'Ce n'est point manquer de respect à Malherbe, ni d'admiration pour son œuvre que de dire : après l'effort violent, tumultueux, désordonné de la Pléiade et de cette foule de poètes qu'elle suscita derrière elle, il était natural que le goût public, un peu fatigué par les hardiesses des novateurs, se montrât disposé à favoriser surtout des qualités toutes différentes : une facture ferme et soutenue dans le vers, fût-elle un peu monotone ; une ordonnance régulière dans la composition, dût le poete y montrer plus de sagesse dans le raisonnement que de vivacité d'imagination ; une langue régulière, sobre et châtiée, tout opposée à l'exubérance de Ronsard et de son école. Malherbe répondit merveilleusement à cette disposition générale des esprits, prêts à goûter paisiblement un excellent écrivain en vers, plutôt qu' à suivre dans les nues un grand poète intempérant.'[1]

In England the poets who marvelously responded to the demands of the change in public taste were those rather insignificant versifiers, Waller and Denham[2]; and to them, accordingly, the credit of the reform was generally given. But, as Dr. Johnson points out, the authority of such naturally minor persons would have been ineffectual without the powerful support of Dryden. Enlisting under the banners of Aristotle, Horace, Ben Jonson, and Corneille, he began a mighty onslaught on the sins of the old poetic diction, and inaugurated at once the modern period of English prose and the age of the heroic couplet. But Dryden's own heedless practice was not the best possible recommendation of 'correctness.' It was not until the patiently

[1] *Histoire* 4. 1. This chapter is by Petit de Julleville himself.
[2] 'After about a half a century of forced thoughts and rugged metres some advances toward nature and harmony had been made by Waller and Denham.'—*Life of Dryden* (*Lives* 1. 419). See *ibid.* 1. 393, notes 1 and 6, for a list of some of the numerous references in the eighteenth century to Denham's strength and Waller's sweetness.

artistic Pope took up the good work that the triumph of the new style was complete. In the development of the art and fame of Pope, and the reaction against Pope, are summed up the whole history of English literature between Milton and Wordsworth. The period ended in a wholesale abolishment of poetic diction, and a return to the spoken language as the source and standard of literary expression. We do not usually recall that it began in exactly the same manner.

1. *The Development of the School of Pope.*

Although Dryden and Pope were later celebrated as the discoverers of those elegances and flowers of speech on which the eighteenth century especially plumed itself,[1] these were an indirect result of their practice, rather than a direct aim of their criticism. The point was not to develop a new poetic diction, but to get rid of an old one; and the attempt was chiefly directed against what all must admit to be vices in any style—careless workmanship, and a system of antiquated words or forms of words which did not correspond to the language as it was actually spoken. In both cases the effort was negative rather than positive, characterized by *Thou shalt nots* rather than by *Thou shalts.*

The desire to avoid careless workmanship—to trust nothing to the caprice of the poet—led to the development of a standard metre, the heroic couplet, which had been a

[1] 'There was, therefore, before the time of Dryden no poetical diction, no system of words at once refined from the grossness of domestic use, and free from the harshness of terms appropriated to particular arts. . . . Those happy combinations of words which distinguish poetry from prose had rarely been attempted; we had few elegances or flowers of speech; the roses had not yet been plucked from the bramble, or different colors had not yet been joined to enliven one another.'—*Dryden* (*Lives* 1. 420).

favorite with Ben Jonson,[1] and had become increasingly popular through the century. The rules for the manipulation of this type of verse became so strict that the art of packing thoughts and feelings of every sort into these neat lines without any apparent difficulty might seem to demand a miracle of ingenuity.[2] In the first place, the poet must close the sense with the couplet. These couplets he must make metrically readable, without departing from the normal character and relation of words in prose. He must invert the order as little as possible,[3] and must avoid the use of words unnecessary to the sense, or forms that had become obsolete. Under this latter type were included the expletive *do*,[4] and the old ending of the second and third person of the present indicative *est*[5] and *eth*. Moreover, the versification must be not only readable, but distinctly melodious to the ear.[6] There must be no hiatus,[7] no wearisome repetition of the same vowel, no clash of

---

[1] 'Aside from his strictly lyrical verse, in which Jonson shared the metrical inventiveness of his age, the decasyllabic rimed couplet was all but his constant measure.' Schelling, 'Ben Jonson and the Classical School,' *Pub. Mod. Lang. Assoc.* 13. 235.

[2] See Pope's letter on versification, *Letters* 1. 56-59.

[3] Cf. the Earl of Musgrave's *Essay upon Poetry* (Spingarn 2. 288):

>   Th' expression easy, and the fancy high,
>   Yet that not seems to creep, nor this to fly;
>   No words transpos'd, but in such just cadence
>   As though, hard wrought, may seem th' effect of chance.

[4] Dr. Johnson censures Waller for using the expletive *do* very frequently, 'though he lived to see it almost universally ejected.'—*Waller* (*Lives* 1. 294). Cf. Pope, *Essay on Criticism* 347. Dryden is not careful to avoid the expletive; there are four examples of it in the first fifteen lines of *Absalom and Achitophel*.

[5] 'He sometimes uses the obsolete termination of verbs,' says Dr. Johnson of Waller, mentioning this as another 'abatement' of his 'excellence in versification.'

[6] Pope, *Essay on Criticism* 364.

[7] *Ibid.* 345: 'Though oft the ear the open vowels tire.' But cf. his remarks on hiatus, *Letters* 1. 58. Pope says that in all Malherbe's poems he found but one example of hiatus.—*Letters* 1. 78.

consonants; the music must be full, clear, and continually varied.[1] The rhyme must be exact,[2] and must fall on naturally accented syllables, not on weak words like *of, to,* etc. If to all these virtues the poet could add the sweetness of alliteration, for which Waller was famed, and the onomatopœic skill displayed by Dryden in his song for St. Cecilia's day, and by Pope in his *Essay on Criticism,* he was in a fair way to escape the censure that awaited the careless craftsman. To be a good craftsman, a thorough master of the technique of rhyming, was the chief ambition of the poets of the new generation. For it they were willing to surrender all claim to those rarer graces that lie beyond the reach of art.

While this emphasis upon correctness and polish in versification naturally led to a similar emphasis in the choice of words, the reform began in France with a notable anticipation of Wordsworth's preference for the language of the lower and middle classes. Of the literary principles of Malherbe, Petit de Julleville writes[3]: 'Elle se réduit à un petit nombre de préceptes, plutôt négatifs; comme de décrire les choses par leur traits les plus généraux; de relever seulement, par une harmonie savante et un habile arrangement, des idées et expressions si simples qu'en des mains moins adroites elles sembleraient purement prosaïques. Cette simplicité presque banale des termes

---

[1] 'T is all we can do to give sufficient sweetness to our language: we must not only choose our words for elegance, but for sound; to perform which a mastery in the language is required; but the poet must have a magazine of words, and have the art to manage his few vowels to the best advantage, that they may go further. He must also know the nature of the vowels, which are more sonorous, and which more soft and sweet.'—Ker 2. 215-216.

[2] See Johnson's remarks on Waller's rhymes.—*Waller* (*Lives* 1. 294). Pope's rhymes were not always exact; see the list of inexact rhymes in the concordance to Pope. Klopstock remarked upon Dryden's carelessness in this respect to Wordsworth, who defended Dryden.—*B. L.* 2. 178.

[3] *Histoire* 4. 9-10.

employés lui faisait dire que "les crocheteurs du Port au Foin étaient ses maîtres en fait de langage."' As Malherbe sought his language among the 'crocheteurs,' the Royal Society in England turned to the language of 'artisans, country-men, and merchants' for clear and effective expression.[1] Although the Royal Society was interested in the simplification of English prose style for the sake of scientific clearness, rather than of artistic beauty, it helped to establish a new ideal. The sins of English prose were the sins of English verse also; and Sprat's criticism of the misuse of ornament in the one was equally applicable to the other.

The ornaments of speech have much degenerated from their original use, writes Sprat.[2] 'They were at first, no doubt, an admirable instrument in the hands of wise men; when they were only employed to describe goodness, honesty, obedience, in larger, fairer, and more moving images, to represent truth clothed with bodies, and to bring knowledge back again to our very senses, from whence it was at first derived to our understandings. But now they are generally changed to worse uses; they are in open defiance to reason, professing not to hold much correspondence with that.' Finding this bad habit of speech utterly at variance with all scientific honesty, the Royal Society 'is most rigorous in putting into execution the only remedy that can be found for this extravagance.' Accordingly it exacts from all its members a 'close, naked, natural way of speaking; positive expressions, clear senses; a native easiness, bringing all things as near the mathematical plainness as they can; and preferring the language of artisans, country-men, and merchants before that of wits and scholars.'

[1] The parallel with the *Lyrical Ballads* is recognized by Professor Raleigh, who comments on the difference in purpose also.—Introduction to the selections from Sprat, in Craik, *English Prose* 3. 270.
[2] Spingarn 2. 117-118.

Of course the language of 'artisans, country-men, and merchants' played little part in the verse of Dryden's day; but a 'natural way of speaking' was religiously cultivated. Every remnant of the older diction which had persisted in poetry, but not in the spoken language, was unconditionally banished. This vehement objection to words and phrases that had become purely literary was due to the causes that inspired a similar reform on the part of Wordsworth. By a judicious combination of the turns of speech especially consecrated to verse, an ignorant or uninspired rhymester could conceal his own lack of invention or skill, and could fill up a line with something which looked like poetry, but was not. The 'dismal slaughter' of this time-honored poetic diction is humorously described by Robert Wolseley in 1685[1]: 'The *eds* went away with the *for tos* and the *untils* in the general rout that fell on the whole body of the *thereons*, the *thereins*, and the *therebys*, when those useful expletives, the *althos*, and those most convenient synalæphas, *'midst, 'mongst, 'gainst, and 'twixt*, were every one cut off; which dismal slaughter was followed by the utter extirpation of the ancient house of the *therebys* and the *therefroms*, etc. Nor is this reformation the arbitrary fancy of a few who wou'd impose their own private opinions and practice upon the rest of their countrymen, but grounded on the authority of Horace, who tells us in his Epistle *De Arte Poetica* that present use is the final judge of language (the verse is too well known to need quoting), and on the common reason of mankind, which forbids us those antiquated words and obsolete idioms of speech whose worth time has worn out, how well so ever they may seem to stop a gap in verse and suit our shapeless immature conceptions, for what is grown pedantic and unbecoming when 't is spoken will not have a jot the better grace for being writ down.'[2]

[1] Spingarn 3. 27.
[2] Malherbe said that 'ce qui est banni du langage, doit l'être de l'écriture.'—Petit de Julleville, *Histoire* 4. 679.

In this attempt to make verse approximate to the spoken language, Dryden even goes so far as to object to any departure in verse from the normal order of words in prose, and particularly condemns a mannerism frequent in the *Female Vagrant*[1] in the first volume of *Lyrical Ballads*—the habit of so inverting the order that the rhyme falls on the verb. 'And therefore I admire that some men should perpetually stumble in a way so easy,' he remarks,[2] 'and, inverting the order of words, constantly close their lines with verbs, which, though commended sometimes in writing Latin, yet we were whipt at Westminster if we used it twice together. I know some who, if they were to write in blank verse, "Sir, I ask your pardon," would think it sounded more heroically to write, "Sir, I your pardon ask."[3] I should judge him to have little command of English whom a necessity of rhyme would force upon this rock; though sometimes it cannot easily be avoided; and indeed this is the only inconvenience with which rhyme can be charged. This is that which makes them say rhyme is not natural, it being only so when the poet makes a vicious choice of words, or places them, for rhyme's sake, so unnaturally as no man would in ordinary speaking; but when it is so judiciously ordered that the first word in the verse seems to beget the second, and that the next, till that becomes the last words in the line which in the negligence of prose would be so, it must then be granted that rhyme has all the advantages of prose, besides its own.' This sounds very much like Wordsworth's suggestion that poetry

---

[1] No joy to see a neighboring house, or stray
Through pastures not his own, the master took;
My Father dared his greedy wish gainsay.
                    —*The Female Vagrant,* lines 41-43.

[2] Ker I. 6.

[3] But compare the preface to the works of Waller, 1690, which expresses the new ideals also. There Waller is praised for giving firmness and point to his lines by closing them with verbs, 'in which we know the life of language consists.'

is only the language of prose with metrical beauty superadded, though every reader must be aware of a subtle difference which cannot now be defined.

Although Dryden did not often succeed in preserving the order of prose in rhymed couplets, he was careful to do so in his blank verse. The result of his attempt may be seen in the following passage from Antony's dying speech to Cleopatra,[1] which has the simplicity and pathos too often lacking in Dryden's dramas:

> But grieve not, while thou stayest
> My last disastrous times.
> Think we have had a clear and glorious day,
> And Heav'n did kindly to delay the storm
> Just till our close of evening. Ten years' love,
> And not a moment lost, but all improved
> To the utmost joys,—what ages have we lived!
> And now to die each other's; and so dying,
> While hand in hand we walk in groves below,
> Whole troops of lovers' ghosts shall flock about us,
> And all the train be ours.

But Dryden did not accept the ideal of Malherbe without question. He made certain modifications which all tended in the direction of greater freedom and expressiveness. Although Malherbe was content with the speech of the 'crocheteurs,' he also believed in the abolishment of all special terms; he would employ only so much of the vocabulary of the porters as was generally intelligible. This, of course, was a good principle, but it was subject to misinterpretation and abuse. On this account Dryden scornfully opposed it. Dr. Johnson, the most notable representative of this French ideal in England, is forced to devote several paragraphs to the refutation of Dryden's statement that the use of general terms[2] serves only to conceal the

---

[1] *All for Love* 5. 1 (*Works* 5. 432).

[2] Of course the type of language opposed to general terms was not specific descriptive adjectives, etc., but the cant terms, the slang of particular professions. But the phrase was often given a wider application.

poet's ignorance—or, in Wordsworth's phrase, makes it unnecessary for him to write with his eye on the object.[1] 'It is a general rule in poetry,' remarks Dr. Johnson, 'that all appropriated terms of art should be sunk in general expressions, because poetry is to speak a general language. . . . Yet Dryden was of the opinion that a sea-fight ought to be described in nautical language, and certainly, says he, "as those who in a logical disputation keep to general terms would hide a fallacy, so those who do it in any poetical description would veil their ignorance."' Dryden adds that he is not ashamed to learn something about language from sailors.[2] Evidently, when he does not write with his eye on the object, his sins are not due to his theory of poetry, but to other circumstances of which we must speak later.

Besides those modifications in the French practice which were due to Dryden's own English common sense, there was always a tendency to reaction in favor of the vigor and freedom of imaginative expression which characterized the elder poets, and which the moderns were fast losing. This was partly responsible for the inconsistency with which Dryden's criticism was often charged. He seemed to find the French ideal somewhat inadequate[3]; and, though he was not the most honorable and admirable of men, as far as moral character was concerned, he had a kind of intellectual honesty. Real contact with the works of his great predecessors, whom he was so ready to refine

---

[1] *Dryden* (*Lives* I. 433). Johnson is quoting from the preface to the *Annus Mirabilis* (Ker I. 13). Of course Dryden changed his mind on this subject, as he did on most others at some time in his life. See Ker, p. xxxiii.

[2] 'If I have made some few mistakes, it is only . . . because I have wanted opportunity to correct them; the whole poem being first written . . . where I have not so much as the converse of any seaman.'—Ker I. 13.

[3] Ker I. 194-195. Note his characteristic remarks on French refinement. 'For my part,' he says, 'I desire to be tried by the laws of my own country.'

and censure,[1] often led to a temporary reaction against the new standard of good sense and regular versification—in his defense of poetic license in the preface to the *Fall of Man*, for example, and in his attempt to recapture some of the richness of the old blank verse in *All for Love*. There is often a kind of wistfulness, as well as a manly and unaffected reverence, in his appreciation of Shakespeare and Milton. He was not altogether unconscious of the ancient liberty and power which were departing from English verse, not to be recovered until the days of Wordsworth. For the loss of this liberty, and the creation of a substitute poetry more obnoxious than all the unpruned growths of the metaphysical imagination, Dryden himself was responsible, as we shall see; but this was largely the indirect result of some deficiencies in his own poetic gifts. His precepts, like his most characteristic practice, were in favor of that selection of the 'language actually used by men' which he called 'plain English.'

But Dryden's blunt, heedless, vigorous spirit was naturally inclined to those very sins against which his criticism was often directed. He knew how to be simple, and simple in so homely and manly a style that one of the first symptoms of the reaction against Pope was a preference for the bolder rhythms and plainer language of Dryden.[2] But he did not know how to be polished:

[1] Dr. Johnson speaks of Dryden's favorite pleasure of discrediting his predecessors. *Dryden* (*Lives* I. 349). A similar complaint seems to have been made in Dryden's lifetime. 'I am made a detractor from my predecessors, whom I do confess to have been my masters in the art,' he writes.—*Ibid.* I. 349, note 4.

[2] In speaking of the advantage of using simple and homely language, Warton says: 'Dryden often hazarded it, and gave by it a secret charm and a natural air to his verses.' As an example, he quotes:

> Sir Balaam now, he lives like other folks,
> He takes his chirping pint and cracks his jokes.
> 'Live like yourself' was now my Lady's word,
> And lo! two puddings smoked upon the board.
> —*Essay* 2. 175.

> Even copious Dryden wanted or forgot
> The last and greatest art, the art to blot.

The importation of this somewhat alien virtue into English verse required an artist of more patience and address. Such an artist was Pope. He completed the work of reforming and refining the literary language by the standard of well-bred conversation in England, somewhat as his master, Boileau, completed the work of Malherbe in France. In his hands the conception of a 'selection of the real language of men' lost the more universal character that Dryden was inclined to give it, and was more regularly associated with the ideal of correctness, and the avoidance of everything vulgar.

Pope, indeed, was just the man to finish such a work, after it had been inaugurated by a man of greater intellectual initiative than he. Although endowed with little originality of mind, he was by nature a poet and an artist— more of a poet, perhaps, than the world was ever permitted to discover, more exclusively an artist than any other English poet. In him the purely artistic impulse seemed to predominate over every other. All his joy and ambition lay in the skilful adaptation of means to the attainment of a desired end. But he readily accepted the end proposed to him by others. In an age which emphasized good sense, he devoted a lifetime to bringing reason and rhyme together.[1] When Walsh told him that the only virtue yet to be attained in English poetry was the virtue of correctness, he determined that, before his death, the English should boast this virtue also. While poets were struggling with an unperfected medium, he demonstrated how brilliantly and easily a mere lad could do what they only tried to do. In his hands the couplet was condensed to the last degree of condensation, and polished to the highest beauty that polish alone can confer. In this delight in skill—in the exercise of it, and the fine and astonishing results of it—lay the secret of his whole activity.

[1] Preface to the *Miscellaneous Works of Pope*, 1716.

But in all this he really made no original modification of what he received from others. The ideal had been completely defined before he adopted it. His criticism, much more than his poetry, is summed up in his own famous words: 'What oft was thought, but ne'er so well express'd.' His criticism, more than his poetry, we say, because in poetry he seems to have possessed a delicate and original vein of his own that in a different age might have made of him a very different poet. In his willingness to let others do his critical thinking for him, he unconsciously stifled impulses which might have resulted in something besides the most airy and subtly malicious of satires. The forms that his imagination took when the carefully clipped wings happen to attain to some brief flight—as in the fairy machinery of the *Rape of the Lock,* or the mediæval background of *Eloisa and Abelard*—reveal a graceful and romantic spirit. He had a gift of pathos, too. Under all the glossy language of *Eloisa and Abelard* and the *Elegy on the Death of an Unfortunate Lady,* there is a real substance of pathetic thought. The impression derived from these deviations from the normal course of satirical and didactic verse is strengthened by numerous instances of his romantic taste in his letters, by his lifelong love of the *Faerie Queene,* and by the quality and music of his early verses on solitude. Had his artistic ambitions and his wonderful skill in imitation been inspired by other models than Waller, and Dryden, and Boileau, England might have lost a sparkling satirist, and gained a lyrical poet.

This Wordsworth always realized. To Pope he never denied what he denied to Dryden—the possession of the true poetic gift. Had Pope trusted more to his native genius, and less to the praise which his boyish display in the pastorals brought him, said Wordsworth, he could never have descended to the position of an immediately popular poet. This descent Wordsworth ascribes to his boyish inexperience when he began to write, and to his inordinate love of praise.¹ Perhaps it may be as justly ascribed to that strong artistic and histrionic instinct which led him to take more delight in a character deliberately adopted or created than in the qualities that were his own. Such a disposition is sufficiently obvious in his plotting life.

However this may be, Pope threw all his artistic ambition into the perfection of the French ideal already naturalized in England by Dryden, and partly suggested to Pope himself by Boileau. This ideal was the Horatian doctrine of a polite and well-bred mean in language as in life. The poet must be familiar, but not vulgar,² carefully avoiding low and rustic expressions on the one hand, and bombast on the other hand, just as a gentleman avoids pomposity and constraint of manner without being coarse or awkward, or failing to do the right thing at the right time. The pleasant ease of the man to the manner born, the elegant and unadorned simplicity of the well-dressed lady—these correspond in life to the ideal of politeness in literary expression. Just as the well-bred man does what the rest of the company are doing, quite naturally and gracefully, never pretending to invent manners and customs for himself; so the poet must use the language that other people talk, giving it only the inconspicuous, yet all-pervading charm of an exquisite propriety in the choice and application of it. This gentlemanly scorn for unseemly ornament is expressed by the youthful Pope in the *Essay on Criticism*.³

> Words are like leaves; and where they most abound
> Much fruit of sense beneath is rarely found.
> False eloquence, like the prismatic glass,
> Its gaudy colors spreads on every place;

[1] *Essay Supplementary to the Preface.*
[2] 'As there is a difference betwixt simplicity and rusticity, so the expression of simple thoughts should be plain, but not clownish.'—Preface to the *Pastorals*.
[3] *Essay on Criticism* 319-333. In a letter to Caryll, Pope gives expression to his preference for simplicity, in terms that are much

> The face of Nature we no more survey;
> All glares alike, without distinction gay.
> But true expression, like the unchanging sun,
> Clears and improves whate'er it shines upon;
> It gilds all objects, but it alters none.
> Expression is the dress of thought,[1] and still
> Appears more decent as more suitable;
> A vile conceit in pompous words expressed
> Is like a clown in regal purple dressed:
> For different styles with different subjects sort,
> As several garbs with country, town, and court.

The difference between this ideal of simplicity and that of Wordsworth is not easy to define. Like the difference between the courtesy of a kindly, well-bred man and the passionate gentleness of a Bernard of Clairvaux, it is not so much a matter of outward conduct as of degrees of intensity and purity in the spirit that suggests and controls the outward action.

In his attempt to attain this urbane simplicity, Pope neither spared the file nor shunned the flames that Horace so mercilessly recommends to young writers. 'With the unwearied application of a plodding Flemish painter, who draws a shrimp with the most minute exactness,' says Cowper,[2] 'he had all the genius of one of the first masters. Never, I believe, were such talents and such drudgery united.' He found as much pleasure in correcting as in writ-

---

more like Wordsworth: 'I have often found by experience that nature and truth, though never so low and vulgar, are yet pleasing when openly and without artifice represented; insomuch that it would be diverting to me to read the very letters of an infant, could it write its innocent inconsistencies and tautologies just as it thought them.'—*Letters* I. 190.

[1] 'Language is the apparel of poesy.'—Sir William Alexander, in Spingarn I. 182. 'Language is the dress of thought.'—*Dryden* (*Lives* I. 58). Wordsworth told DeQuincey that it was highly unphilosophical to call language the 'dress of thought.' He would call it the 'incarnation of thought.'

[2] Cowper, *Letters* 4. 168-169.

ing,[1] and not in correcting once, but many times. 'After writing a poem, one should correct it all over with one single view at a time,' he told Spence.[2] 'Thus for language, if an elegy,—"these lines are very good, but are they not in too heroical a strain?"' 'In translating both the *Iliad* and the *Odyssey* my usual method was to take advantage of the first heat; and then to correct each book, first by the original text and then by other translations; and lastly to give it a reading for the versification only.'[3] But after he had thus used the file, he did not always spare the application of the flames. 'I have prevented not only many mean things from seeing the light, but many which I thought tolerable. For what I have published I can only hope to be pardoned; but for what I have burned I deserve to be praised.'[4]

The result of this unwearied effort was that, within the sphere which he had made his own, he set an example of fine and conscientious wordmanship that might be applied with advantage to other types of poetry. But this sphere was a very limited one. When he carried the ideal of 'what oft was thought, but ne'er so well expressed' outside of the field of experience of which he himself was a proper judge, the badness of the thought or the lack of thought was made only more pernicious by that polished grace with which he uttered it. Nothing could be more different, for instance, than Pope's 'interiors' and his 'landscapes'—to borrow terms from painting. The simplicity, the exactness, the use of familiar and specific terms to designate familiar and specific things, in the first, are only equaled by the glossy vagueness of the second. As an example of this difference we may compare the reference to

---

[1] 'I corrected because it was as pleasant for me to correct as to write.'—Preface to the *Miscellaneous Works of Pope* 1716.
[2] *Spence's Anecdotes*, p. 270.
[3] *Ibid.*, p. 23.
[4] Preface to the *Miscellaneous Works*.

> The darksome pines that o'er yon rocks reclined
> Wave high, and murmur to the hollow wind,
> The wandering streams that shine between the hills,
> The grots that echo to the tinkling rills,
> The lakes that quiver to the curling breeze,[1] etc.

with the following;

> In the worst inn's worst room, with mat half-hung,
> The floor of plaister, and the walls of dung,
> On once a flock-bed, but repaired with straw,
> With tape-tied curtains, never meant to draw,
> The George and Garter dangling from the bed
> Where tawdry yellow strove with dirty red,
> Great Villiers lies.[2]

If, as Joseph Warton said, with a disapproving glance at some of Pope's work, 'The use, the force, and the excellence of language certainly consists in raising clear, complete, and circumstantial images, and in turning readers into spectators,'[3] Pope often succeeds in writing very forcibly and excellently. It is in this malicious choice and assemblage of specific and characteristic circumstances, in the airy simplicity with which he calls a spade a spade, that his power as a satirist lies. This power, of which he gives so few illustrations in landscape and ideal 'historical' painting, is always conspicuous in his genre pictures. He does not name or characterize the blossoms in a 'flowery mead'; but he does name the contents of Belinda's toilet-table. The tasks of the shepherds in the pastorals are indicated in the vaguest terms, but the game of cards in the *Rape of the Lock* is described in all its complicated technical details. In Wordsworth's pathetic use of 'natural little circumstances' in his narrative of the ruined cottage, he is putting to nobler uses the art of being specific which he might have learned from Pope, or from Pope's disciple, Goldsmith.

[1] *Eloisa to Abelard* 155-160.
[2] *Moral Essays* 3. 299-305.
[3] *Essay* 2. 165.

This enormous difference in Pope's style when he is dealing with different types of subject-matter suggests the real origin and character of the poetic diction to which Wordsworth objected. It also shows how inseparably the new style of the *Lyrical Ballads* was connected with a new poetic substance. As long as Dryden and Pope were dealing with their own proper material—the life that they themselves knew—there is little in their style or their theory of style that is in essential disagreement with that of Wordsworth. They were quite as insistent as he upon the necessity of writing as unaffected persons talk, and of avoiding all special literary diction. In emphasizing this, they rendered a permanent service to English style by establishing a literary standard of grammar and syntax which really corresponded to the normal structure of the spoken English sentence. It is this clear and natural structure that makes Dryden's prose seem modern. It gives an appearance of ease and lucidity to the vaguest and most periphrastic verse of the century. One reason why Wordsworth, with all his natural tendency to involved and peculiar syntax, can write so clearly, is that the despised eighteenth century had preceded him, and had not preached grammar and correctness for a hundred years for nothing. An excellent clearness and simplicity of diction, as well as of grammar, are characteristic of Pope's generation. Toward the end of the century Cowper, complaining that 'simplicity is become a very rare quality in a writer,' remarks[1]: 'Swift and Addison were simple; Pope knew how to be so, but was frequently tinged with affectation; since their day I hardly know a celebrated writer who deserves the character.' At another time, in words which anticipate Coleridge's definition of Wordsworth's ideal, he writes[2]: 'To make verse speak the language of prose without being prosaic—to marshal the words of it in such an order as they might

[1] Cowper, *Letters* 4. 323.
[2] *Ibid.* 4. 176.

naturally take in falling from the lips of an extemporary speaker, yet without meanness, harmoniously, elegantly, and without seeming to displace a syllable for the sake of rhyme, is one of the most arduous tasks a poet can undertake. He that could accomplish this task was Prior.' Where could we turn for better examples of verse which speaks the language of prose without losing its own proper charm, than to the beginning of the eighteenth century—to the sparkling *bons mots* of Pope, the colloquial negligence of Prior, the *naïveté* and occasional tenderness of Gay, and even the 'close, naked, natural way of speaking' that Swift carried into rhyme from his prose? But beyond their own limited field their taste and imagination become less sure, and various elements corrupt the bright simplicity.

In the first place, there is the universal ignorance of or indifference to natural phenomena, combined with the artistic ambition to do what other poets had done before them, and do it better. The beauty of the external world has always held an important place in poetry, because men in general are interested in it. Storm and sunshine, the clouds and the stars above our heads, and the familiar flowers at our feet, have been the universal and permanent background of all human experience, and are inevitably associated with the memory and expression of it. Poets sing the 'glories of the rolling year' as naturally as we all begin a social conversation with a remark about the weather. Hence a generation which was interested in writing good and effective verse, but whose own experience was mainly associated with the streets of London, naturally made use of this traditional matter of poetry; but, since it was used as a traditional element for the sake of an artistic effect, and was not brought to the test of experience by either the writer or the reader, the consequence was that the style in which these things were described was usually affected by the lack of genuine knowledge and feeling behind the style. Sometimes, when Wordsworth condemns the language of his predecessors, he is referring only to the falsity of the substance. It is as easy to tell a lie in the language of the lower and middle classes as in the language of the court. Bad descriptions of nature were not always written in phraseology in itself gaudy and inane.

This, perhaps, is true of the famous description by Dryden which Wordsworth particularly condemns[1]:

> All things are hushed as Nature's self lay dead;
> The mountains seem to nod the drowsy head.
> The little birds in dreams their songs repeat,
> And sleeping flowers beneath the night dews sweat.
> Even Lust and Envy sleep; yet Love denies
> Rest to my soul, and slumber to my eyes.[2]

Here is no poetic diction. The language is simple, concrete, and touching. The only trouble is that it does not tell the truth. No one who ever really saw the solemn outlines of the mountains at night could write or enjoy the second verse. Yet the lines are, in some respects, so artistic that it is not difficult to see how such writing as this could lull not exceedingly vigilant powers of observation to sleep along with the drowsy mountains, and could encourage lesser mortals to imitate the falsehood, where they could not rival the art. Just as the moonlight on our gaudy modern stage, flooding trees and flowers that are like no trees and flowers that ever grew, somehow produces an effect analogous to that produced by the peace and silvery beauty of actual moonlight, so these words suggest the quiet and loneliness of the sleeping world. The effect of any given passage depends on much besides the truth of the separate details. The cadence, the associations of the words, the various arts of repetition and emphasis, have all their own share in the general impression. In this case, for instance, the mind under the spell of the soft flow of the metre and the refrain-like recurrence of the word *sleep*

[1] *Essay Supplementary to the Preface.*
[2] *The Indian Emperor* 3. 2 (*Works* 1. 360).

and its synonyms, is as little inclined to question the drowsiness of the mountains as it is to inquire how these plural mountains came to be provided with only one head. It is only a counterfeit poetry, cheating the unwary; but it has an artful appearance of 'nature and simplicity.'

But Dryden himself seems to have been unable to distinguish the genuine metal of poetry from the gilded substitute, at least in his own productions—as a glance at the example of imaginative boldness that he cites in the Preface to the *Fall of Man* will show.[1] His critical instinct was right, but his imaginative feeling was not. 'I admire his talents and genius highly,' wrote Wordsworth to Scott,[2] when Scott was getting out his edition of Dryden, 'but his is not a poetical genius.[3] The only qualities I can find in Dryden that are essentially poetical are a certain ardor and impetuosity of mind with an excellent ear. It may seem strange that I do not add to this great command of language; that he certainly has, and of such language too, as it is most desirable that a poet should possess, or rather that he should not be without. But it is not language that is, in the highest sense of the word, poetical, being neither of the imagination nor of the passions—I mean of the amiable, the ennobling, or the intense passions. I do not mean to say that there is nothing of this in Dryden, but as little, I think, as is possible considering how much he has

---

[1] He cites the following as his own most successful attempt to imitate the imaginative boldness of Milton:
> Seraph and cherub, careless of their charge,
> And wanton, in full ease now live at large:
> Unguarded leave the passes of the sky,
> And all dissolved in hallelujahs lie.

This, he says, is imitated from Virgil: *Invadunt urbem, somno vinoque sepultam.* 'A city's being buried is just as proper an occasion as an angel's being dissolved in ease and songs of triumph!'—Ker I. 188.

[2] *L. W. F.* I. 208-210.

[3] Wordsworth agrees with Milton, who said Dryden was a good rhymist, but no poet.—Preface to Newton's *Milton*, p. 8.

written. You will easily understand my meaning when I refer to his versification of *Palamon and Arcite*,[1] as compared with the language of Chaucer. Dryden has neither a tender heart nor a lofty sense of moral dignity. Whenever his language is poetically impassioned, it is mostly on unpleasing subjects, such as the follies, vices, and crimes of men or of individuals. That his cannot be the language of imagination must have necessarily followed from this: that there is not a single image from nature in the whole body of his works; and in his translation from Virgil, whenever Virgil can be fairly said to have his eye on the object, Dryden always spoils the passage.'[2] Although Dryden was not essentially a poet, his energy and even grandeur of mind, the natural swiftness and fire which were really intellectual qualities, but which often simulated the glow of real passion, together with a remarkable facility, enabled him to produce an excellent substitute for poetry. This seemed to be quite satisfactory to an age

---

[1] Wordsworth's statement may be illustrated by comparing the lines,

> Arcite, false traytour wikke!
> Now artow hent, that lovest my lady so,
> For whom that I have al this peyne and wo,
> And art my blood, and to my counseil sworn.
> * * * * * *
> I wol be deed, or elles thou shalt dye,
> Thou shalt not love my lady Emelye,

with Dryden's version, where struggling tenderness has wholly given way to self-complacent and oratorical wrath:

> False traitor, Arcite, traitor to thy blood,
> Bound by thy sacred oath to seek my good,
> Now art thou found forsworn for Emily,
> And darest attempt her love for whom I die.
> * * * * *
> Hope not, base man, unquestioned hence to go,
> For I am Palamon, thy mortal foe.

[2] As an illustration of this compare *Æneid* 4. 522-527 with Dryden's version.

which had lost the old gift of song, and was cutting itself off from the springs of imaginative feeling in nature and common life.

It was due to this natural lack of at least one type of imaginative feeling, rather than to any theory of poetic diction, that Dryden became the creator of the elegances and flowers of speech so dear to the heart of the eighteenth century, so obnoxious to the taste of the nineteenth. As far as can be discovered from his numerous prefaces, his only purpose with respect to language was to give as clear and correct and melodious a reproduction of the current speech as possible. If his ambition occasionally soared higher, it showed itself only in the wistful effort to write with some of the splendor and spirit of his less refined predecessors. Hence the falsity of such a description as that just quoted seems to be due to some unconscious blindness, rather than to deliberate intention. The same is true of the elegant phrases which Dr. Johnson takes to represent a new achievement in verse. Most of them are singularly uninteresting; but, for some reason, they took hold of the poetical imagination of his successors. For instance, there is the adjective 'watery.' 'To him the ocean is a "watery desert," a "watery deep," a "watery plain," a "watery way," a "watery reign." The shore is a "watery brink," or a "watery strand." Fish are a "watery line," or a "watery race." Sea-birds are a "watery fowl." The launching of ships is a "watery war." Streams are "watery floods." Waves are "watery ranks." The word occurs with wearisome iteration in succeeding poets.'[1] Such mannerisms seem to be due to the heedlessness of a man writing with great facility, but ignorant of, or indifferent to, the phenomena he mentions. He seizes upon the most obvious, and, at the same time, the most matter-of-fact and uninteresting detail, and then, when he perceives the

[1] Myra Reynolds, *The Treatment of Nature in English Poetry*, p. 39.

necessity for varying his expression, he acts like the clever writer that he is rather than the sympathetic observer that he is not: instead of mentioning a new detail, he merely thinks of a synonym for the expression that he has already used. In this way all the tiresome array of stock phrases that mean nothing came into being. Most of them ring monotonous changes upon the most obvious features of things, such as the fact that the ocean is composed of water, that birds have feathers and fish have fins. To call fish the 'finny race' is not to say anything new or interesting about them; to vary the expression to the 'scaly tribe' is only to make matters worse. Yet it is easy to see that all these atrocities might be produced, with no intention of thus distinguishing poetry from prose, by any man who was trying to write well without knowing what he was talking about. In fact, the same kind of diction occurs in prose which attempts to deal with the same kind of subject-matter.

These two characteristics of Dryden's treatment of natural phenomena—the perversion of the facts for the sake of heightening a single impression, and the use of set phrases indicating, as Wordsworth said, nothing more than the knowledge that a blind man could pick up concerning the familiar but ever-changing aspects of Nature—these vicious tendencies were also strengthened by the gallantry of Waller and his imitators, who made all the mighty powers of earth and sky subservient to the glory of some fair lady or some all-powerful nobleman.

> In praising Chloris, moons, and stars, and skies,
> Are quickly made to match her face and eyes—
> And gold and rubies, with as little care,
> To fit the color of her lips and hair;
> And, mixing suns, and flowers, and pearl, and stones,
> Make them serve all complexions at once.[1]

'At the death of any illustrious man or fair lady all nature was convulsed with grief. When Cælestia died the rivu-

---
[1] Butler, *Satire on a Bad Poet;* quoted by Miss Reynolds, p. 31.

lets were flooded by the tears of the water-gods, the brows of the hills were furrowed by new streams, the heavens wept, sudden damps overspread the plains, the lily hung its head, and birds drooped their wings. When Amaryllis had informed nature of the death of Amyntas, all creation "began to roar and howl with horrid yell." When Thomas Gunston died just before he had finished his seat at Newington, Watts declared that the curling vines would in grief untwine their amorous arms, the stately elms would drop leaves for tears, and that even the unfinished gates and buildings would weep. In love-poetry nature is frequently represented as abashed and discomfited before the superior charms of some fair nymph. Aurora blushes when she sees cheeks more beauteous than her own. Lilies wax pale with envy at a maiden's fairness. When bright Ophelia comes, lilies droop and roses die before their lofty rival. So the sun, when he sees the beautiful ladies in Hyde Park,

> Sets in blushes and conveys his fires
> To distant lands.

And when that modest luminary is aware of the presence of the fair Maria, he

> Seems to descend with greater care;
> And, lest she see him go to bed,
> In blushing clouds conceals his head.

Nature is thus constantly compelled into admiring submission to some Delia or Phyllis or Chloris. Even further than this do the poets go. They make all the beauty of nature a direct outcome of the lady's charms. In the gardens at Penshurst the peace and glory of the alleys was given by Dorothea's more than human grace. No spot could resist the civilizing effect of her beauty. . . .
The extravagance of speech stood as the sign of an intensity of feeling that did not exist. The poet was not swept away by overwhelming passion. He worked out his verses with conscious deliberation. A lady-love was one of the

necessary poetical stage-properties, so the poet cast about him for a Phyllis or an Amoret, and then cast about him for something to say to her. Such lines as Waller's on Dorothea, who is so much admired by the plants that

> If she sit down, with tops all tow'rds her bow'd,
> They round about her into arbours crowd:
> Or if she walks in even ranks they stand,
> Like some well marshalled and obsequious band,

are at once felt to be merely cold, tasteless hyperbole. The lines do not win a second's suspension of disbelief. Modes of speech, a conception of nature, such that high-wrought emotion might justify it, or that might be natural and inevitable when the poet's thought was ruled by a living mythology, became mere frigid conventionalities when there was no passion, and when the spirits of stream and wood no longer won even poetic faith.'[1] This easy method of praising a mistress is also humorously described by Ambrose Philips:

> To blooming Phyllis I a song compose,
> And, for a rhyme, compare her to a Rose;
> Then, while my fancy works, I write down Morn,
> To paint the blush that doth her cheek adorn,
> And, when the whiteness of her skin I show,
> With extasy bethink myself of Snow.
> Thus, without pains, I tinkle in the close,
> And sweeten into verse insipid prose.[2]

As long as these exaggerations were confined to the celebration of fair ladies they had perhaps some artistic justification. No doubt the poet knew that he was not telling the truth; and most certainly the lady knew it. Even the reader was in the secret. It was all a poetic fiction, a graceful convention, and imposed on no one. As such, the poet was entitled to vary and elaborate it as

---

[1] Myra Reynolds, *The Treatment of Nature in English Poetry*, pp. 33-35.
[2] Ambrose Philips, quoted by Miss Reynolds, p. 32.

cleverly as he could. But this easy manipulation of all the mighty frame of Heaven and earth, of the changeless stars and the wayward winds, to suit the purposes of every gallant poetaster, served, like Dryden's rhetoric about the 'drowsy mountains,' to cultivate an indifference to the facts. Scribblers soon fell into the way of telling the same kind of falsehoods when there was no reason for so doing, and this despite their inability to do it as cleverly as their unscrupulous masters—though perhaps they did not know that. We shall have an example of the ridiculous results of this habit later.

But meanwhile it is obvious that, in all this fine writing, dulness of vision is often matched by deadness of heart. And this brings us to Wordsworth's second indictment against the language of the period. It is heartless, he says. Here again the real fault is something greater and deeper than the choice of a certain type of vocabulary; but it resulted, almost unconsciously, or at least unintentionally, in the habits of speech that became poetic diction. Uncontrolled by a true sensitiveness of heart, the language of passion (which is the language of poetry) suffered the same fate that attended the natural imagery. As the clever writer varied his descriptions, not by adding a new detail, but by finding a new synonym, so he varied the metaphorical delineation of feeling, not by recurring to the original emotion, but by finding parallel and analogous expressions for what had already been said by himself or some other poet. It was a process of building bricks without straw. When he did go abroad for his material, he naturally went to the writers that preceded him, especially to the Latin writers. There he could find the best material from Nature already selected and arranged—poetically pre-digested, as it were. Why should he confuse himself, and waste time and energy, re-examining the original crude and unmethodized source, when poets that he could trust had already done so, and had reported upon what they had seen? Why should he not devote his talents to improving the use of what they had chosen? To us Blair's statement[1] that Milton's *L'Allegro* and *Il Penseroso* were storehouses of natural imagery from which all later poets had drawn, immediately suggests the question: But why did they not go to the greater storehouse that lay at their very doors? Why did they not merely do as Milton had done—take a walk some fine morning, and tell what they saw? How could they dream of assuming the dignity of poets merely by 'descriptions copied from descriptions, by imitations borrowed from imitations, by traditions, imagery and hereditary similes, by readiness of rhyme and volubility of syllables.' But, after all, the fault lay neither with the habit of imitation, nor with the laudable ambition to write well from which this habit proceeded. Pope's *Imitations of Horace* are not lacking in originality or appropriate simplicity of language. Within their own proper field all these ideals of expression, which we are so ready to condemn, worked excellently. The fact that the poets of the age were less successful in the wider fields beyond was partly their fault, but partly also their misfortune. When they ventured away from the familiar streets and polite circles of London, they left behind them 'the hearing ear and the seeing eye,' and the feeling heart also. And without these even the standards of Wordsworth would be useless.

To the type of diction that inevitably developed where poets lacked the touchstone of personal observation and genuine feeling, Pope made some special contributions of his own. Since he really had a better eye for natural beauty, and more romantic tenderness of feeling, than some of his predecessors, his imagery is often more exact, and his language of passion less frigid than theirs. In him we rarely find the shameless and absolute prevarications of which Dryden and Waller were capable. Yet his sins in this respect were bad enough. His motto—which, to fit his

---

[1] Blair, *Essays on Rhetoric*, p. 319.

case, may be varied to 'What oft was tried, but ne'er so well performed'—often led him to commit all the sins of his age. The result is a singular unevenness. In one line of the *Pastorals* he remarks, quite gracefully and simply,[1] 'Now hawthorns blossom and now daisies spring'; in another he inanely announces[2]:

> The turf with rural dainties shall be crown'd,
> While opening blooms diffuse their sweets around.

In *Windsor Forest* we find such couplets as these[3]:

> See Pan with flocks, with fruit Pomona crown'd,
> Here blushing Flora paints the enamell'd ground,
> Here Ceres' gifts in waving prospect stand,
> And nodding tempt the joyful reaper's hand.

But these are shortly followed by descriptions of tolerable concreteness:[4]

> See! from the brake the whirring pheasant springs,
> And mounts exulting on triumphant wings:
> Short is his joy; he feels the fiery wound,
> Flutters in blood, and panting beats the ground.
> Ah! what avail his glossy varying dyes,
> His purple crest, and scarlet-circled eyes,
> The vivid green his shining plumes unfold,
> His painted wings, and breast that flames with gold?

But, even in the passage where he is employing this more concrete language, we notice an artificiality in the style, which proves, upon closer analysis, to consist mainly in the habit of balancing one half of the line against the other. 'Now hawthorns blossom' exactly balances 'now daisies spring'; 'See Pan with flocks' is paralleled by 'with fruit Pomona crown'd'; and 'his purple crest' is paired with 'scarlet-circled eyes.' This antithesis is often achieved at the expense of truth and grammar. 'I could

---

[1] *Spring* 42.
[2] *Ibid.* 99-100.
[3] *Windsor Forest* 37-40.
[4] *Ibid.* 111-118.

never get the blockhead to study his grammar,' said Swift. In the line, 'See Pan with flocks, with fruit Pomona crown'd', he suggests that Pan is crowned with flocks.

Even Eloisa has enough self-possession for a few neat antitheses. 'I mourn the lover, not lament his fault,' she says, adding very shortly:[1]

> How happy is the blameless Vestal's lot!
> The *world forgetting,* by *the world forgot:*
> Eternal sunshine on the spotless mind!
> *Each prayer accepted,* and *each wish resign'd;*
> Labor and rest that equal periods keep;
> Obedient slumbers that can wake and weep;
> *Desires composed, affections ever even;*
> *Tears that delight,* and *sighs that waft to heaven.*

This mannerism was emphatically condemned by Wordsworth as one of the worst features of the style of Pope: 'These intellectual operations (while they can be conceived of as operations of the intellect at all, for in fact one half of the process is mechanical, words doing their own work and one half of the line manufacturing the rest) remind me of the motions of a posture master, or of a man balancing a sword upon his finger which must be kept from falling at all hazards. . . . Why was not this simply expressed without playing with the reader's fancy, to the delusion and dishonour of his understanding, by a trifling epigrammatic point?'[2]

When to the regular antitheses and epigrammatic points of Pope were added the flowers and elegances of speech already invented by Dryden and Waller, and when the unscrupulous falsification of the obvious facts of nature was encouraged by a popular objection to everything 'vulgar,' the poetic diction which Wordsworth was later to

---

[1] *Eloisa to Abelard* 207-212.
[2] See Wordsworth's detailed analysis of an epitaph by Pope, in *Upon Epitaphs,* Part 2, *Wordsworth's Literary Criticism,* pp. 118-122.

abolish was already fairly well developed. But the theory of it was not. While it was everywhere stated that poetry must be refined, there is, with the single exception of a notable utterance by Addison, to be quoted later, virtually no evidence for belief that verse should be distinguished from prose, or from cultivated conversation of the same 'refined' type, by a special vocabulary or licenses of grammar and syntax. In 1700 Wordsworth's declaration that there neither is nor ever can be any essential difference between the language of prose and the language of verse would probably have seemed less strange than it seemed in 1800.

As far as difference was recognized, it is the difference that Wordsworth himself was willing to concede. Poetry, being the language of passion, naturally reproduces the peculiarities of emotional speech in a freer syntax and order of words, and in a more highly figurative expression, than is necessary in prose. This was especially emphasized, though not happily illustrated, by Dryden,[1] who derived his ideas from Longinus, and by John Dennis, who, more than any other critic of the time, often anticipates Wordsworth's point of view.

One other distinction was commonly made: poetry, even more than prose, must speak a general language, a language intelligible to all. A failure to perceive in what the universality of language consists led to the monstrous doctrine that poetry must employ only general terms. This principle, so unhappily applied in the eighteenth century, was later adopted by Wordsworth and Coleridge, with very different results, as we shall see.

Moreover, criticism in the early eighteenth century was not wholly blind to the merits of a simplicity that was not also refined. Steele liked the directness and concreteness of unlearned colloquial speech[2]; Addison remarks that

[1] Ker 1. 185-186.
[2] *Guardian* 23. Cf. Hamelius, *Die Kritik in der Englischen Literatur des 17. und 18. Jahrhunderts*, p. 99.

there is more in common between the plain language of the popular ballads and the majestic simplicity of Virgil, than between the style of Virgil and that of such fanciful writers as Cowley[1]; Pope thinks that he would like even the style of an infant if it could write down its thoughts with all their innocent redundancies just as they come[2]; Swift doubts the wisdom of the boasted reform of the language after the Restoration, and thinks that only the influence of the Bible and the Prayer Book upon the speech of the simple people keeps the English tongue from utter degeneracy.[3] These are only temporary reactions, perhaps, but they are not without significance.

Hence it may be seen that the criticism of the period was not the source of the false ideals which Wordsworth and Coleridge were later to combat. The age of Pope did not develop the conception of a special language for poetry, although it almost unconsciously produced such a language. For the theory of a special diction for poetry we must search among the confused and various utterances of the generation succeeding Pope, and almost unconsciously beginning to react against him.

2. *The Reaction Against Pope.*

In the period between the publication of *Paradise Lost* and the appearance of the *Seasons,* the criticism and the practice of poetry had been of a definite and self-consistent character. To draw positive conclusions concerning it is not difficult. But this can hardly be said of the rest of the century. There is a breaking up of the old criticism, without a very definite formulation of a new. The only notable exception to this statement is Joseph Warton's *Essay on the Genius and Writings of Pope.* Warton stands

---

[1] *Spectator* 70.
[2] *Letters* 1. 190.
[3] *A Proposal for Correcting, Improving, and Ascertaining the English Tongue* (*The Prose Works of Jonathan Swift* 2. 15).

fairly and squarely for an ideal of poetic expression in all essential respects different from the practice, if not from the criticism, of the early eighteenth century; and his brave rebellious remarks in 1756 become the source of the most vital discussion of poetic style for the next fifty years, and lead directly to the reform of Wordsworth. But the opinions of the other critics are more difficult to classify. Doctor Johnson, the great exponent of the so-called classical ideal, is as loud in his objection to the 'exploded deities' of Greece and Rome as he is Latinized in vocabulary; and he insists upon a respect for the usual grammar and forms of spoken discourse in verse as warmly as he defends the use of general terms, and the elegances and flowers of speech. Johnson's disciple, Goldsmith, recommends the heroic couplet and the device of personification,[1] while all his own natural sympathies and his own practice are in favor of a pathetic and even homely simplicity unknown to the polished generation of Pope, to which he looks back with some regret. On the other hand, Gray, 'who was at the head of those who, by their reasonings have attempted to widen the space of separation betwixt prose and metrical composition,'[2] was also the centre of a new and regenerative influence which revealed itself in a more picturesque imagery, and a free and beautiful cadence, in the later poetry of the century.

Since this is so, it will be well simply to quote the notable individual utterances on poetic diction, and then proceed to examine the result of the rather chaotic ideals of the century as revealed in the average verse of Wordsworth's own time—the sort of verse that was appearing in the magazines of 1796.

Since the 'poetic diction' of the English Augustan age was the outcome of the practice, rather than the deliberate theories, of Dryden and his followers, the expression of the

[1] *On Metaphors* (*Works* I. 373).
[2] Preface to the *Lyrical Ballads*.

new ideal consisted mainly in an attack upon the verse of Pope, and the formulation of principle opposed to his practice—in Warton's *Essay on the Genius and Writings of Pope*. This essay is the immediate source of some of Wordsworth's most famous remarks. Warton goes to the heart of the matter at once[1]: 'All I plead for is . . . to impress on the reader that a clear head and acute understanding are not sufficient alone to make a poet; that the most solid observations on human life, expressed with the utmost elegance and brevity, are *morality*, and not poetry; that the epistles of Boileau in rhyme are no more poetical than the character of La Bruyère in prose; and that it is the creative and glowing *imagination, acer spiritus ac vis*, and that alone, that can stamp a writer with this exalted and very uncommon character which so few possess, and of which so few can properly judge.'

Having thus suggested where Pope belongs, Warton proceeds to point out the falsity of most of the contemporary descriptions of external nature. It is strange that in the pastorals of a young poet there should not be 'one rural image that is new,'[2] but this, he fears, must be said of Pope.[3] With Pope's treatment of the seasons he compares that of Thomson[4]: 'Thomson was blessed with a strong and copious fancy; he hath enriched poetry with a variety of new and original images, which he painted from nature itself, and from his own actual observations; his descriptions have, therefore, a distinctness and truth, which are utterly wanting to those of poets who have only copied from each other, and have never looked abroad on the

[1] *Essay* I. iv-v.
[2] Cf. Wordsworth, *Essay Supplementary to the Preface:* 'Now it is remarkable that, excepting the Nocturnal Reverie of Lady Winchelsea, and a passage in the Windsor Forest of Pope, the poetry of the period between the publication of Paradise Lost and the Seasons does not contain a single new image from external nature.'
[3] *Essay* I. 2.
[4] *Ibid.* I. 41-47.

objects themselves. Thomson was accustomed to wander away into the country for days and for weeks, attentive to "each rural sight, each rural sound," while many a poet who has dwelt for years on the Strand has attempted to describe fields and rivers, and generally succeeded accordingly. Hence that nauseous repetition of the same circumstances; hence that disgusting impropriety of introducing what may be called a set of hereditary images, without proper regard to the age, or climate, or occasion in which they were formerly used. . . . If our poets would accustom themselves to contemplate fully every object before they attempted to describe it, they would not fail of giving their readers more new images than they generally do.'[1]

Not only does he object to the falsity and vagueness of imagery in the poetry of the eighteenth century; he is also disposed to scoff at stilted refinement, and to recommend language more natural and touching. He praises as 'pathetic to the last degree' the lines from *Jane Shore:*

> Why dost thou fix thy dying eyes upon me
> With such an earnest, such a piteous look,
> As if thy heart were full of some sad meaning
> Thou couldst not speak,

adding that the few words, 'Forgive me, *but* forgive me' in this play exceed the most pompous declamation of *Cato*.[2]

Of course Warton's criticism was not only the cause but the effect of a change in taste. Everywhere there were indications of this change—of an increasing interest in nature and common life and the romantic past beyond the age of refinement. Almost all the poetry of note in the generation preceding Wordsworth heralded his coming, and gave the impulse to his genius. But Joseph Warton is especially noteworthy, as clearly and distinctly formulating

---

[1] Cf. Wordsworth, Preface to the *Lyrical Ballads:* 'I have at all times endeavored to look steadily at my subject; consequently there is, I hope, in these poems little falsehood of description.'

[2] *Essay* I. 273-274.

the new ideal which was variously illustrated in the poems of Thomson, Goldsmith, Cowper, and even Gray.

Warton's good work was carried on by a much less intelligent person—John Scott of Amwell, who is of interest to us because his *Essays* were read by Wordsworth in his youth. Although his remarks are vitiated by a rather undiscriminating emphasis on what he believes to be 'correctness,' he insists, even more earnestly than Warton, on clear and characteristic imagery; and he has no mercy on the old periphrastic diction. 'Blushing Flora,' he says,[1] 'is the quaint and indistinct language of a schoolboy; for why Flora should blush no good reason has ever been discovered.'

But while the criticism was thus undermining the influence of the poetic diction, the conception of a special usage for poetry, which had been incidentally suggested by Addison, began to become widespread.

3. *Theories of Poetic Diction.*

The theory of a special diction for poetry was the result of the emphasis placed by Dryden and Pope upon the selective power of the poet, and upon the value of imitation. The poet must employ the current speech, but he must also avoid everything vulgar or unintelligibly specific. Moreover, he was permitted, even advised, to incorporate into his verse the happiest inspirations of his predecessors. The result was the development of the notion that there is a special language of poetry—a treasure of fine phrases descending from bard to bard, and especially consecrated to the uses of the imagination. In general, the term poetic diction was applied only to these 'happy combinations' of words. Transpositions of words from the order of prose, the coining of new words, the use of strange forms, etc.,

---

[1] *Essays on the Writings of Several English Poets*, p. 72.

were all condemned by men like Dr. Johnson and Goldsmith, who represent the purest classical ideal in this respect, and whose criticism is echoed in the reviews of Wordsworth's day.

But there was a less popular conception of the special language of poetry which permitted a slight departure from the strictness of prose in the matter of vocabulary and syntax, provided this did not obscure the intelligibility of the verse. Of this conception Addison's analysis of the style of Milton, according to the standards of Aristotle, is perhaps the best example.

Hence there arose two types of poetic diction, representing the classic and the romantic traditions—if we may employ those vague but convenient terms. The one, imitating the example of Dryden and Pope, retained the grammar and syntax, and, for the most part, the vocabulary of prose, but employed the happy combinations of words recommended by Dr. Johnson; the other, imitating Milton and Spenser, the poetic models in the reaction against Pope, rejected the phrases and versification of the heroic couplet, but made use of the old words and 'licentious transpositions' so emphatically condemned by Dr. Johnson and the reviewers. The various modifications of this ideal of a special language for poetry may be seen in the following typical quotations:

    1. Addison[1]: If clearness and perspicuity were only to be consulted, the poet would have nothing else to do but to clothe his thoughts in the most plain and natural expressions. But since it often happens that the most obvious phrases, and those which are used in ordinary conversation, become too familiar to the ear, and contract a kind of meanness by passing through the mouths of the vulgar, a poet should take particular care to guard himself against idiomatic ways of speaking. . . . Milton has but few failings in this kind, of which, however, you may meet with some instances, as in the following passages:

[1] *Criticisms of Paradise Lost,* ed. Cook, pp. 21-23.

> Embryos and idiots, idiots and friars,
> White, black, and gray, with all their *trumpery*
> Here pilgrims roam.
> . . . . .
> A while discourse they hold,
> No *fear lest dinner cool*—when thus began
> Our author.
> . . . . .
> Who of all ages to succeed, but feeling
> The evil on him brought by me, will curse
> My head? Ill fare our ancestor impure,
> For *this we may thank Adam.*

The great masters in composition know very well that many an elegant phrase becomes improper for a poet or an orator when it has been debased by common use. . . . . The judgment of a poet very much discovers itself in shunning the common roads of expression, without falling into such ways of speech as may seem stiff and unnatural; he must not swell into the false sublime by endeavoring to avoid the other extreme.

Addison then proceeds to enumerate the ways by which, according to Aristotle, the language of verse may be distinguished from that of prose, and illustrates them by reference to *Paradise Lost.* They are:

1. The use of metaphor. (But the poet is not to have recourse to this when the proper and natural words will do as well.)

2. The use of idioms of other tongues. 'Under this head may be reckoned the placing the adjective after the substantive, the transposition of words, the turning the adjective into a substantive, with several foreign modes of speech which this poet has naturalized to give his verse the greater sound, and throw it out of prose.'

3. Use of several old words or words newly coined (*miscreated, hell-doomed,* etc.).

However, Addison believes that Milton has taken these liberties rather too frequently, and has thereby stiffened and obscured his style. But he admits that this license is perhaps more necessary in blank verse than in rime. 'Rime, without any other assistance, throws the language off from prose.'

2. Gray[1]: The language of the age is never the language of poetry; except among the French, whose verse, where the thought and image does not support it, differs in nothing from prose. Our poetry, on the contrary, has a language peculiar to itself, to which almost every one that has written has added something by enriching it with foreign idioms and derivations: nay, sometimes words of their own composition or invention. Shakespeare and Milton have been great creators this way; and no one more licentious than Pope or Dryden, who perpetually borrow expressions from the former. Let me give you some instances from Dryden, whom every one reckons a great master of our poetical tongue:—full of *museful mopings,* unlike the *trim* of love, a pleasant *beverage,* a *roundelay* of love, stood silent in his *mood,* with knots and *knares* deformed. . . . . But they are infinite; and our language not being a settled thing (like the French) has an undoubted right to words of a hundred years old, provided antiquity have not rendered them unintelligible. In truth, Shakespeare's language is one of his principle beauties. . . . . Every word in him is a picture.

3. Johnson[2]: Language is the dress of thought; and as the noblest action or the most graceful action would be degraded and obscured by a garb appropriated to the gross employments of rustics or mechanics, so the most heroic sentiments would lose their efficacy, and the most splendid ideas drop their magnificence, if they are conveyed by words used only upon low and trivial occasions, debased by vulgar mouths, and contaminated by inelegant applications. Truth is indeed always truth, and reason is always reason; they have an intrinsic and unalterable value, and constitute that intellectual gold which defies destruction: but gold may be so concealed in baser matter that only a chemist can recover it; sense may be so hidden in unrefined and plebeian words that none but philosophers can distinguish it.

There was therefore before the time of Dryden no poetical diction: no system of words at once refined from the grossness of domestic use, and free from the harshness of terms appropriated to particular arts. Words too familiar or too remote defeat the purpose of the poet. From those sounds which we hear on small or on coarse occasions we do not easily receive strong impressions or delightful images; and words to which we are nearly strangers,

---

[1] *Letter to Richard West,* April 4, 1742 (*Letters* 1. 98).
[2] *Life of Cowley* (*Lives* 1. 58); *Life of Dryden* (*Lives* 1. 420).

whenever they occur, draw that attention to themselves which they should transmit to things. Those happy combinations of words which distinguish poetry from prose had been rarely attempted; we had few elegances or flowers of speech.

4. Goldsmith[1]: It is indeed amazing, after what has been done by Dryden, Addison, and Pope, to improve and harmonize our native tongue, that their successors should have taken so much pains to involve it into pristine barbarity. These misguided innovators have not been content with restoring antiquated words and phrases, but have indulged themselves in the most licentious transpositions, and the harshest constructions, vainly imagining that the more their writings are unlike prose, the more they resemble poetry; they have adopted a language of their own, and call upon mankind for admiration. All those who do not understand them are silent, and those who make out their meaning are willing to praise to show they understand. From these follies and affectations the poems of Parnell are entirely free; he has considered the language of poetry as the language of life, and conveys the warmest thoughts in the simplest expression.

The various opinions here so strongly expressed were weakly echoed in the average criticisms of the last decades of the century—in Blair's *Essays on Rhetoric,* for example, and in the *Critical Review.* It became a truism that 'our language has a special diction for poetry'; but this special diction was usually definitely limited by the taste of the critic, and of the particular poets whom he chose to regard as models. The followers of Spenser and the followers of Pope each regarded the poetic diction of the other as entirely without justification, and were inclined to appeal to the standard of spoken language to reënforce their arguments. But meanwhile Burns and Cowper had been silently preparing the way for another ideal—the one by employing the language of the lower and middle classes in his own land, and the other by illustrating his own ideal of expression—'to make verse speak the language of prose without being prosaic, to marshal the words of it in such an order as they might naturally take in falling from the

[1] *Life of Thomas Parnell* (*Works* 4. 173).

lips of an extemporary speaker, yet without meanness, harmoniously, elegantly, and without seeming to displace a syllable for the sake of rhyme.'

4. Poetic Diction in 1796-1797.

But, as Coleridge says, in order to understand the reform of Wordsworth, we must also make ourselves acquainted with the sort of verse that was appearing when he began to write. It happens that some of the most typical examples of such verse are to be found in the *Monthly Magazine*, which was also publishing the revolutionary efforts of Coleridge and his friends. Apart from the productions of these young innovators, and apart also from a few deliberate imitations of Cowper and Collins and Gray, this verse divides itself into two types, or two variations upon one type. The difference consists in the versification rather than the language.

On the one hand, we find examples of the heroic couplet and all the periphrastic elegances associated therewith. Of this type the following translation from Lucretious is a good example:

> For thee the fields their flowery carpet spread,
> And smiling Ocean smooths his wavy bed;
> A purer glow the kindling poles display,
> Robed in bright effluence of ethereal day,
> When through her portals bursts the gaudy Spring,
> And genial Zephyr waves his balmy wing.
> First the gay songsters of the feather'd train
> Feel thy keen arrows thrill in every vein.[1]

On the other hand, we find a large number of effusions in verse which, without materially differing from this specimen in language, reveal the influence of Collins, Gray, and the Wartons in a sweeter and freer versification borrowed chiefly from Milton's minor poems. These poems (if poems they may be called) are characterized by a slightly simplified, though hardly more specific, diction, and by a

[1] February, 1797.

rather unconvincing tone of melancholy and love of natural scenery. However, this love does not lead the authors to a very careful or intimate observation of the objects of their affection. For the most part, they, too, are content with the old inanities about balmy spring and all her monotonous zephyrs. The following are specimens of this ameliorated verse. The first is a rather favorable example of the results of the new interest in Milton's minor poems:

> Oh, far removed from my retreat
> Be Av'rice and Ambition's feet!
> Give me, unconscious of their power,
> To taste the peaceful, social hour.
> Give me, beneath the branching vine,
> The woodbine sweet, or eglantine,
> When evening sheds its balmy dews,
> To court the chaste, inspiring Muse.[1]

Here there is a complete absence of the periphrastic diction of the first example, though the imagery is still a little conventional. But such echoes of Dyer and other imitators of *Il Penseroso* are less frequent than verses like the following, in which the old words are fitted to new tunes:

> See, fairest of the nymphs that play
> In vernal meadows, blooming May
>   Comes tripping o'er the plain.
> Lo! All the gay, the genial powers
> That deck the woods or tend the flowers
>   Compose her smiling train.[2]

>   To *a Primrose.*
> Pale visitant of balmy spring,
>   Joy of the new-born year,
> Thou bidst young hope new plume his wing
>   Soon as thy buds appear.
> While o'er the incense-breathing sky
>   The tepid hours just dare to fly,
> And vainly woo the chilling breeze,[3] etc.

[1] February, 1797.
[2] April, 1797.
[3] *Ibid.*

Now and then we find examples of natural imagery that is not only hopelessly general but absolutely false—the falseness consisting in the unnatural personification displayed most conspicuously in those eighteenth-century verses in honor of 'nymphs' before whom lofty trees bow in reverence, and roses blush to find their beauties rivaled by the 'lovely fair.' The bad habits inculcated by this extravagant gallantry lead poetasters into the most ridiculous falsifications—even when they are celebrating a Nature that does not suffer from competition with these distracting goddesses. In the following effusion the coming of the sun (Apollo) is described in the terms formerly used of the advent of some lovely lady or dazzling lord:

> See! As he comes, with general voice,
> All nature's living tribes rejoice,
>   And own him as their king;
> Ev'n *rugged rocks their heads advance,*
> *And forests on the mountains dance,*
>   *And hills and valleys sing.*[1]

Such verse in a magazine of good character gives point to Wordsworth's rather sarcastic reference to the school of good sense: 'I have at all times endeavored to look steadily at my subject; consequently there is, I hope, in these poems little falsehood of description, and my ideas are expressed in language fitted to their respective importance. Something must have been gained by this practice, as it is friendly to one property of good poetry, namely, good sense.'

This latter type has been quoted at some length to show that M. Legouis is hardly correct in saying[2] that the influence of the landscape school was responsible for the poetic diction against which Wordsworth's efforts were directed. This poetic diction he describes as consisting in those deviations from the order and syntax of prose which he finds in Wordsworth's own early work. But, obviously, the one

---

[1] June, 1797.
[2] *The Early Life of William Wordsworth*, pp. 127-134.

thing that is not characteristic of contemporary verse is this departure from the ordinary usage of spoken language, either with respect to grammar or choice of words, if we regard the words separately, and not in combination. Of course there are a few examples of harsh constructions, such as the imitation of the ablative absolute, rather common in the poetry of the later eighteenth century, and never wholly discarded by Wordsworth. But, for the most part, the grammar and syntax are correct and easy—as may be seen by looking back at the examples already quoted. In the first example there is a slight departure in the first, third, and fifth lines from the strict order of prose; but we do not feel the inversion to be so awkward as it is in the lines from Wordsworth cited by M. Legouis. Moreover, the grammatical construction is quite simple and regular. In the second extract only the clause, 'Give me to taste,' seems rather unusual in the spoken language. In the next two poems, however, the order is strictly that of prose, and, apart from the word 'incense-breathing,' there is not a word which might not be heard in fairly cultivated conversation. This, with one or two exceptions, is true of the other verses. On the whole, one could hardly expect in any age to find verse of the average character which was less unmusical, or more simple and clear in construction, or which employed fewer words not heard in ordinary speech. That these characteristics are typical may be seen by any reader who takes the trouble to examine the miscellanies and magazines of the day. The boast of the eighteenth century that it had at last made English verse metrically and grammatically correct is borne out by such an examination.

What then is it that removes the language of this verse so far from nature and truth—for obviously this is not the way in which sensible men express themselves? While sensible men use these words separately, they do not use these combinations of them. They may employ the words *genial, waves, balmy,* and *wing,* at different times and for different purposes, but, in order to indicate that a soft and gentle breeze is blowing, they do not say that 'genial Zephyr waves his balmy wings.' In other words, the poetic diction consists, not in the separate words, but in those 'happy combinations' which, as Dr. Johnson says, distinguish poetry from prose. The peculiarity of these elegances of speech is that they suggest an image, not by using the word or words associated with it in everyday experience, but by using, in its stead, another image associated with it only in verse—a kind of accepted symbol for the image. Hence, instead of the clear and coherent pictures suggested simply by a list of the common names of the phenomena that actually occur together in nature—green grass, sunshine, and violets, for instance,—we are given a heterogeneous mass of substitute images, which cannot be actually visualized without somewhat ridiculous results. To such an end had one attempt to make the language of verse approximate to the language of typical conversation arrived! Yet it must not be forgotten that there had been such an attempt, even at the basis of this monstrous development.

From this long review it may be seen that, on the whole, the authors of the *Lyrical Ballads* were justified in believing that their theory and practice were in accordance with the best traditions of English poetry. It may also be seen that the question of poetic diction was exceedingly complicated, because it involved not only matters of vocabulary and grammar, but the far more difficult problems of rhetoric, and the ultimate basis of rhetoric in human psychology. The special contribution of Wordsworth and Coleridge consisted in their recognition of these problems of psychology, and the insight and personal experience which they brought to bear upon them. The bold young poets of the *Lyrical Ballads* were merely restating an old proposition; but the terms of the restatement were so striking, and the illustrations so original, that the old ideal seemed like a discovery of their own. But how they themselves happened to make the rediscovery we have yet to learn.

CHAPTER 3.

WORDSWORTH'S POETIC DEVELOPMENT PREVIOUS TO THE MEETING WITH COLERIDGE.

To trace the different paths by which the vigorous and independent mountain-lad, and the dreamy but sociable young philosopher of Christ's Hospital, arrived at the same ideal of simplicity is not one of the least interesting of literary inquiries. It is the more interesting because simplicity was as little characteristic of the natural genius of the one as of the other. The only poet of the age who was normally as self-conscious and elaborate as S. T. Coleridge was William Wordsworth. And yet, as Wordsworth said,

> Though mutually unknown, yea, nursed and reared
> As if in several elements, we were framed
> To bend at last to the same discipline,
> Predestined, if two beings ever were,
> To seek the same delights, and have one health,
> One happiness.[1]

The final character of this discipline was determined as much by the youthful development of Coleridge as by that of Wordsworth; but since Wordsworth is, as it were, the hero of this tale, we must begin with his early experiments in poetry and criticism, and use those of Coleridge only as supplementary and illustrative material.

Wordsworth's literary career was rather precocious. He was something of a critic before he was ten, and a really skilful maker of verses at the age of fourteen.[2] But even before this he had unconsciously begun to lay the founda-

[1] *Prelude* 6. 254-259.
[2] *The Idiot Boy* 337-338.

tion of his future theory of poetry in those curious imaginative experiences described in the *Prelude*. No one who lives among the grand and lonely forms of nature is free from a touch of primitive superstition—from a tendency to start at the sudden rustling of leaves in a forest, or to feel a strangeness in the blowing of the wind, or the motion of the sky above some unfrequented mountain-height. The facing of these inexplicable but unconquerable fears was the grand adventure of Wordsworth's boyhood. Sometimes he was ignominiously vanquished by them, as in that nocturnal experience when he seemed to feel the dark shape of the mountain at night stride after him 'with measured motion like a living thing,' and 'with trembling oars' rowed back to the safe covert of the willow.[1] More often they entered suddenly into his consciousness in the midst of the excitement of some physical exploit:

> Oh! when I have hung
> Above the raven's nest, by knots of grass
> And half-inch fissures in the slippery rock
> But ill sustained, and almost (so it seemed)
> Suspended by the blast that blew amain,
> Shouldering the naked crag, oh, at that time
> While on the perilous ridge I hung alone,
> With what strange utterance did the loud dry wind
> Blow through my ear! the sky seemed not a sky
> Of earth—and with what motion moved the clouds![2]

To the haunting sense of strangeness in his contact with nature were added many other dim and undetermined feelings. Long afterwards, in his talks with Coleridge among the Quantock Hills, the memory of these threw a sudden light upon the old question of the character and source of poetic pleasure, showing him that the poet might be, as nature had been to him, the 'teacher of truth through joy and through gladness'—a creator of 'the faculties by

[1] *Prelude* I. 357-400.
[2] *Prelude* I. 330-339.

a process of smoothness and delight.'¹ This early delight had been manifold in its character. Sometimes it was only an eager and inquisitive interest in the actual forms and appearances of things, a physical delight almost as pure as it was violent. Sometimes it was a dim, half-pagan sympathy with life in all things—

> a sense sublime
> Of something far more deeply interfused,
> Whose dwelling is the light of setting suns,
> And the round ocean and the living air,
> And the blue sky, and in the mind of man,²

rising at times into a still contemplative consciousness of a world beyond the world of sense—of something which had power to make our 'noisy years seem moments in the being of the eternal Silence'³—in the light of which all the solid material universe seemed to become a dream, a prospect in the mind. He was familiar, too, with the magical works of light and storm and mist and darkness among the hills. He says of the mountain shepherd:

> When up the lonely brooks on rainy days
> Angling I went, or trod the trackless hills
> By mists bewildered, suddenly mine eyes
> Have glanced upon him distant a few steps,
> In size a giant, stalking through thick fog,
> His sheep like Greenland bears; or, as he stepped
> Beyond the boundary line of some hill-shadow,
> His form hath flashed upon me, glorified
> By the deep radiance of the setting sun:
> Or him have I descried in distant sky,
> A solitary object and sublime,
> Above all height! like an aerial cross
> Stationed alone upon a spiry rock
> Of the Chartreuse, for worship.⁴

---

[1] Letter to the Friend, *Wordsworth's Literary Criticism*, p. 68.
[2] *Lines composed a Few Miles Above Tintern Abbey*, 95-99.
[3] *Intimations of Immortality* 159-160.
[4] *Prelude* 8. 262-275.

And such phenomena, produced by natural causes, had all the power of a supernatural experience over the heart of the imaginative boy, glorifying and transfiguring the commonest things of every day with the light of visions and strange dreams. Later, the transfiguration was a conscious act of his own imagination, stimulated as it was by much reading among fairy tales and 'old romances.'[1] A 'diamond light,' shed by the setting sun upon a wet rock in front of the cottage, would make the boy's fancy as restless as itself:

> 'T was now for me a burnished silver shield
> Suspended over a knight's tomb, who lay
> Inglorious, buried in the dusky wood:
> An entrance now into some magic cave
> Or palace built by fairies of the rock.[1]

These transports and pure delights of his boyhood, and the renovation of spirit due to his memory of them and return to them, must have been recalled in the memorable conversations which gave rise to the *Lyrical Ballads*. It then occurred to the two friends that the effect of poetry was quite analogous to the effect of these visionary appearances of nature—that it was the function of the poet to fix and retain for ever these momentary exaltations which were as fleeting as the phenomena which occasioned them. Thus poetry—such an enshrining of these experiences as *The Daffodils, The Solitary Reaper,* or *Stepping Westward*—might become what these memories were to Wordsworth, a fountain of refreshment to which he returned again and again:

> There are in our existence spots of time,
> That with a distinct pre-eminence retain
> A renovating virtue, whence, depressed
> By false opinion and contentious thought,
> Or aught of heavier or more deadly weight,

[1] Cf. *Prelude* 8. 406-420.

> In trivial occupations, and the round
> Of ordinary intercourse, our minds
> Are nourished and invisibly repaired;
> A virtue, by which pleasure is enhanced,
> That penetrates, enables us to mount,
> When high, more high, and lifts us up when fallen
> This efficacious spirit chiefly lurks
> Among those passages of life that give
> Profoundest knowledge to what point, and how,
> The mind is lord and master—outward sense
> The obedient servant of her will.[1]

But this noble theory of imagination, which was the basis of the new style of the *Lyrical Ballads,* was also the fruit of conscious experiment during the fourteen years of literary apprenticeship, and of a still longer period of critical reading. Every reader of Wordsworth's own account of himself as one of a band of active, noisy lads, whose year span through a giddy round of hunting, fishing, skating, and all the amusements of country schoolboys, must feel his early achievements of this sort to be rather remarkable. But his father had cultivated his ear for verse, while he was a little child, by making him learn passages from Shakespeare, Spenser, and Milton,[2] and had furnished him with a 'golden store of books,'[3] to which he always returned, in his vacations from school, with tempestuous delight. His love of reading even rivaled his love of fishing—robbing him of some brief holiday sport, and leading him to waste the precious hours, every minute of which he probably had planned with all the foresight and economy of a boy home for a vacation:

> How often in the course
> Of those glad respites, though a soft west wind
> Ruffled the water to the angler's wish,
> For a whole day together, have I lain

[1] *Prelude* 12. 208-223.
[2] *Memoirs* 1. 34.
[3] *Prelude* 5. 479.

> Down by thy side, O Derwent! murmuring stream,
> On the hot stones, and in the glaring sun,
> And there have read, devouring as I read,
> Defrauding the day's glory, desperate!
> Till with a sudden bound of smart reproach,
> Such as an idler deals with in his shame,
> I to the sport betook myself again.[1]

When he was scarcely ten years old, this joy in reading began to develop into a conscious delight in metrical language, and he had learned to select from the passages his father taught him, and the possibly more gaudy verse he chose for himself, the lines and phrases that pleased him for their loveliness or pomp. He draws a charming picture of himself and a 'dear friend' circling the lake in a dewy early morning before any one was abroad, and repeating their favorite verses aloud with one voice, as happy, he says, as the birds whose songs accompanied them. This performance would often last 'for the better part of two delightful hours.' One is tempted to inquire whether the ten-year-old Wordsworth had already memorized enough verse to last through a two-hour recitation, or whether he said his favorites over and over.[2]

However this may be, his favorites were not such as his maturer taste approved:

> And, though full oft the objects of our love
> Were false, and in their splendour overwrought,
> Yet was there surely then no vulgar power
> Working within us,—nothing less, in truth,
> Than that most noble attribute of man
> Though yet untutored and inordinate,
> That wish for something loftier, more adorned,
> Than in the common aspect, daily garb,
> Of human life. What wonder, then, if sounds
> Of exaltation echoed through the groves!
> For, images, and sentiments, and words,

[1] *Prelude* 5. 480-490.
[2] *Ibid.* 5. 552 ff.

And everything encountered or pursued
In that delicious world of poesy,
Kept holiday, a never-ending show,
With music, incense, festival, and flowers!¹

There could be no nobler tribute than this to the false ideals of poetic ornament which he was later to combat! But all the poetic ideals of the eighteenth century seem to have influenced Wordsworth in succession. One reason why his development is so interesting is that, unlike Coleridge and Lamb, he found his poetic inspiration, and the seeds of a progressive growth toward the ideal he was eventually to adopt, chiefly in the literature that was popular in the age preceding him. Beginning as a disciple of Pope, he proceeds, through an interest in the landscape-poets, to all the sins of the revolutionary young writers of his own day. He therefore seems to represent in himself a whole period of literary development.

1. A Disciple of Pope.

Perhaps some of the 'several thousand' lines from Pope which Wordsworth could repeat long after his attack on Pope's language had begun to prove successful,² helped to swell his youthful recitations; for in his first attempt at verse at the age of fourteen he shows himself to be a very clever pupil of the school of the heroic couplet. 'I was called upon, among other scholars,' he said, 'to write verses upon the completion of the second centenary from the foundation of the school [at Hawkshead] in 1585, by Archbishop Sandys. The verses were much admired, far more than they deserved, for they were but a tame imitation of Pope's versification, and a little in his style. This exercise, however, put it into my head to compose verses from the impulse of my own mind, and I wrote, while yet a school-

---
¹ *Prelude* 5. 569-583.
² *L. W. F.* 3. 122.

boy, a long poem running upon my own adventures, and the scenery of the country in which I was brought up. The only part of that poem which has been preserved is the conclusion of it, which stands at the beginning of my collected Poems.'[1] Although, as far as poetic substance and originality are concerned, the *Lines written as a School Exercise at Hawkshead*[2] deserve Wordsworth's disparaging remarks, the apparent ease with which he manipulates the metre, without transgressing the numerous rules laid down by the critics of the eighteenth century, is remarkable. Few passages of verse produced in the palmy days of the couplet show so very little variation from the ideal standard, already described in these pages, as this effort of the country schoolboy. There is no unnecessary expletive in the whole production, and hardly a single example of hiatus[3]; no wrenching of the accent, no unusual form of a word. The rhymes are all exact, with the exception of 'driven' and 'heaven,' and 'grove' and 'move,'[4] which are usual in the heroic couplet. There are only two alexandrines,[5] and no triplets. Moreover, the construction of the sentences is clear, and shows less departure from the normal order of prose than is common in this type of verse; for, despite Dryden's strictures, there was always a tendency to invert the order in a line, in such a way that the rhyme fell on the verb—a mannerism which was considered by some an elegant improvement. There is a natural break

---

[1] *Memoirs* I. 10-13.

[2] Reprinted in the Oxford edition, pp. 618-619.

[3] 86: 'And learn from thence *thy own* defects to scan' is an exception. Wordsworth was always careful to avoid hiatus—more careful than most poets of the nineteenth century, to whose ears it was less offensive than the poets of the preceding century felt it to be.

[4] 1-2, 13-14.

[5] 40, 62. In both cases the alexandrine is used with some climactic effect at the end of a period.

at the end of every couplet. This easy, though somewhat oratorical, style may be illustrated by the following extract[1]:

> No jarring monks, to gloomy cell confined,
> With mazy rules perplex the weary mind;
> No shadowy forms entice the soul aside,
> Secure she walks, Philosophy her guide.
> Britain, who long her warriors had adored,
> And deemed all merit centred in the sword;
> Britain, who thought to stain the field was fame,
> Now honour'd Edward's less than Bacon's name.
> Her sons no more in listed fields advance
> To ride the ring, or toss the beamy lance;
> No longer steel their indurated hearts
> To the mild influence of the finer arts;
> Quick to the secret grotto they retire
> To court majestic truth, or wake the golden lyre.

2. *A Disciple of the Landscape-School.*

About this time Wordsworth's newly awakened poetic ambition received an impulse which resulted in something better than this facile reproduction of the conventionalities of the heroic couplet, and the empty and gaudy imagery associated with it. On the way between Hawkshead and Ambleside, he happened to notice the darkening boughs and leaves of an oak-tree, outlined clearly and strongly against the sunset sky. Like so many of the things that he happened to see for himself, the discovery of this change in the familiar appearance of things, wrought by the evening light, came to him with the freshness and power of a great revelation. 'The moment was important in my poetical history; for I date from it my consciousness of the infinite variety of natural appearances which had been unnoticed by poets of any age or country, so far as I was acquainted with them; and I made a resolution to supply, in some degree, the deficiency. I could not have been at that time

[1] 49-62.

above fourteen years of age.'[1] The direction thus given to his imaginative energies seems to have determined his choice of reading, and the nature of his experiments in verse, until the end of his schooldays. Then the 'still, sad music of humanity' entered his poetry as an even deeper and more powerful impulse than this first vision of the marvels of the external world.

The first result of this discovery of his own powers seems to have been a style of much grace and simplicity, which gradually developed into a morbid peculiarity of expression, and was regained only by a deliberate effort. The only examples of this earlier purity of diction that we have are the extract, 'Dear Native Regions,' mentioned by Wordsworth in the remark just quoted apropos of the *School Exercise;* the sonnet *Written in very Early Youth;* and the *Lines written while sailing in a Boat,* which with the *Remembrance of Collins* originally formed one piece. None of these survives in its original form. For this reason M. Legouis,[2] comparing them with the 'genuine samples' of Wordsworth's early work, supposes their simplicity to be entirely the result of later correction. They are 'early poems only in respect of their subject-matter,' he says. This might seem probable—on the supposition that Wordsworth had but one early style—if it were not for two important circumstances.

In the first place, Wordsworth prints the first two as *Juvenile Poems,* along with the *Evening Walk* and the *Descriptive Sketches;* and, with his usual scrupulous honesty, prefixes to the group the following note[3]: 'Of the Poems in this class, the *Evening Walk* and *Descriptive Sketches* were first published in 1793. They are reprinted with some alterations that were chiefly made very soon after their publication. It would have been easy to amend them,

[1] *Memoirs* I. 67-68.
[2] *The Early Life of William Wordsworth,* p. 121.
[3] *The Miscellaneous Poems of William Wordsworth* [1820] I. 64.

in many passages, both as to sentiment and expression, and I have not been altogether able to resist the temptation, as will be obvious to the attentive reader, in some instances; these are few, for I am aware that attempts of this kind are made at the risk of injuring those characteristic features which, after all, will be regarded as the principal recommendations of juvenile poems.' When he is tempted into further alterations he adds to this comment a further qualification[1]: 'This notice, which was written some time ago, scarcely applies to the Poem "Descriptive Sketches," as it now stands. The corrections, though numerous, are not, however, such as to prevent its retaining with propriety a place in the class of Juvenile Pieces.' But in neither of these notes does he mention the poems which M. Legouis considers early only in respect to subject-matter. Hence he must have considered his corrections so slight and unimportant as not to detract in the least from their original character. It is inconceivable that a man who applies the term 'Juvenile Poems' with such scrupulous accuracy should have silently included under that title pieces that were early in substance only, not in style.

Moreover, it is not difficult to determine approximately the degree of alteration in the case of these poems. At least, a detailed study of the nine different versions can leave very little doubt in the mind of the one who makes the examination, though it is not very easy to condense the results into a convincing proof.

In the first place, these nine versions may be classified as follows:

1. A poem of fourteen lines in octosyllabic couplets, preserved in:

(a) The group of juvenile pieces, printed in the edition of 1815, and reprinted with alterations in the editions of 1820, 1827, 1832, 1836, 1841, and 1845.

---

[1] *The Poetical Works of William Wordsworth* [1836] 1. 46.

(b) A manuscript version reprinted by Knight from a notebook containing parts of *Laodamia, Artegal and Elidure, Black Comb,* the Dedication of *The White Doe,* etc. (*Wordsworth's Poetical Works* 6. 365).

2. The paraphrase in blank verse of the original poem in *Prelude* 8. 467-475.

So many different versions, all purporting to represent the original production, do suggest that the only permanent element in the poem is the subject-matter. But a closer examination simplifies the matter. The variations are then discovered to affect less than half the poem, and to be limited, for the most part, to a wavering choice between two possibilities. One source of the two possibilities then becomes obvious. An original poem in octosyllabic couplets was paraphrased in blank verse for the *Prelude;* and the alterations suggested by the attempt to avoid rhyme, and to expand tetrameters into pentameters, were then experimentally transferred to the original, and, in some cases, finally rejected. The result is that the latest version, which now stands at the beginning of Wordsworth's collected works in the Oxford edition, probably represents the earliest form as well as any except the first printed version (1815). The doubtful lines in it may be easily indicated, and the extent of the doubt determined, by a comparison of this with the paraphrase in the *Prelude,* and with the other versions.

1. The Final Version (that of 1845). (The doubtful words or phrases are printed in italics.)

> Dear native regions, I foretell,
> From what I feel at this farewell,
> *That, whereso'er my steps may tend,*
> And whenso'er by course shall *end,*
> If in that hour a *single* tie
> Survive of local sympathy,
> My soul will cast the backward view,
> The longing look alone on you.

> Thus, while the *Sun sinks down* to rest
> *Far in the regions* of the west,
> Though to the vale no parting *beam*
> *Be given, not one memorial gleam,*
> A lingering *light* he fondly throws
> On the dear hills where first he rose.

2. *The Prelude* 8. 468-475.

> Dear native Regions, wheresoe'er shall close
> My mortal course, there will I think on you;
> Dying, will cast on you a backward look;
> Even as this setting sun (albeit the Vale
> Is nowhere touched by one memorial gleam)
> Doth with the fond remains of his last power
> Still linger, and a farewell lustre sheds
> On the dear mountain-tops where first he rose.

A glance at these two versions shows that the greater part of the poem seems to be quite stable. It remains unaltered in all the various editions, and is reproduced in the *Prelude* as exactly as the metre will permit. This unchanging portion may be taken to represent the part of the original that clearly survives. If it did differ from the original, Wordsworth could have hardly concealed the fact through so many editions. A nervous uncertainty about the wisdom of his own alterations often led him to keep recurring to the earlier form of a poem in later versions; and, in the case of a juvenile poem, this tendency would be increased by a scrupulous fear of dishonestly departing from the youthful style. Hence, where he contentedly writes down the same words, with never a change or a qualm of conscience, for seven different editions, it may be assumed that no other form of these changeless lines is present in his consciousness. Where he does alter, he is likely to alter more than once, and the obvious fluctuation generally reveals the existence of another form in his own mind, and sometimes a character of that form also.

Since so much of the final version seems to represent the original, we might be justified in taking it as characteristic of Wordsworth's youthful style without further ado. But if some of the lines in italics can be proved to be less doubtful than they seem, this corroboration of our judgment will be welcome. Perhaps the best way to decide this will be to examine the questionable phrases one by one.

1. Line 3. The only reason for doubting this verse, and the two other words in this stanza printed in italics, is furnished by the manuscript version, in which lines 3 and 4 read:

> That, when the close of life draws dear [*sic*],[1]
> And I must quit this earthly sphere,

and in which *tender tie* occurs instead of *single tie*. In all the printed versions, the first eight lines are as they stand in the last edition. The relation of these two variants to each other, and to the original, cannot be determined. Since neither of the rhyme-words occurs in the blank verse, and since the word *close* does occur there as well as in the manuscript version, it is not unlikely that *close* originally stood for *end*, and that the couplet had a different rhyme. This is the more likely because there is nothing in the blank verse which seems to stand for the line, *whereso'er my steps may tend*. This might have been added to furnish a rhyme for *end*, if the rhyme of the couplet was altered from an earlier form upon which the passage in the *Prelude* was based. Concerning the variants, *tender* and *single*, no conclusion can be drawn. *Tender* looks like one of those experimental and not very happy changes that Wordsworth often made upon second thought, only to return at last to his original inspiration. Whatever may be the truth concerning the slight variations in the first eight lines, however, they do not seriously affect the character and style of the poem.

[1] Is this a misprint for which Professor Knight, not Wordsworth, is responsible?

2. Lines 9-12 underwent more change than any other part of the *Extract*. In the edition of 1815 they stood as follows:

> Thus when the Sun, prepared for rest,
> Hath gained the precincts of the West,
> Though his departing radiance fail
> To illuminate the hollow Vale.

All the versions except the last present slight modifications of this phraseology; but the instability of the various grammatical relations in virtually the same group of words seems to indicate that there was something in the construction of the original with which Wordsworth was not quite satisfied. This opinion is strengthened by the fact that line 11 is incomplete in the manuscript version, where it is written, *Though no . . . can fail.* Perhaps the truth is that the original rhyme-words were *fail* and *vale,* and Wordsworth, after struggling in vain to remove some blemish without altering the rhyme, finally imported the beautiful phrase *memorial gleam* from the blank verse, and changed the other line in the couplet to correspond with it. It is very likely that the word *precincts* stood for the word *regions* in line 10, since this occurs in all the other versions. Perhaps, on the whole, the lines in the edition of 1815 come as near the original as any. In any case, the same idea and the same group of words seem to be present in all the versions until, in the final edition, the puzzling twelfth line is materially changed.

3. In lines 13-14, the variants represent the temporary influence of the blank verse. In the editions 1820-1840 the last line reads: *On the dear mountain-tops where first he rose,* and in 1832-1840 *lustre* is substituted for *light.* In both cases the change in metre in the blank verse may have made necessary the change from a monosyllabic word, which was then transferred for a time to the original version. The last line in the passage from the *Prelude* is obviously the original tetrameter expanded to a pentameter

by the easy substitution of *mountain-tops* for *hills*. When, therefore, we find that the octosyllabic poem sometimes ends with this decasyllabic line, we may consider it a temporary intruder; and believe that the first printed version, the manuscript version, and the last version, represent the original when they read:

> A lingering light he fondly throws
> On the dear hills where first he rose,

as opposed to

> A lingering lustre fondly throws
> On the dear mountain-tops where first he rose,

which so obviously echoes the blank verse. Hence the more simple and pathetic form, in this case, seems to be the original.

The result of this examination seems to be: (1) that, of the words in italics, *light* and *hills*, and probably *single*, represent the original; (2) that in two of the couplets there may have been a different rhyme, and a corresponding difference in phraseology; and (3) that, while the rhymes in lines 9-10 seem to be permanent, there is a slight variation otherwise. If we are right in supposing that the part of the poem which shows no fluctuation probably survives substantially as it was first written, these changes really affect its essential character very little. Of course it may be said that the comparison of a poem of 1786, first printed in 1815, with a paraphrase probably written between 1799 and 1805, but not printed until 1850, does not give very trustworthy evidence concerning the original style. For aught we know, the passage in the *Prelude* may have been remodeled in accordance with the printed version of 1815. But since, in all the public appearances of the production, there is no trace whatever of a form essentially different from the form printed by Wordsworth as a juvenile poem, there seems to be no reason for doubting the word of so honest a man. The burden of proof certainly rests upon those who presume to question the statement of the poet.[1]

What has been said concerning the *Extract* applies almost equally to the *Sonnet Written in Early Youth*. The absence of the fluctuation characteristic of the selections from the descriptive poems which Wordsworth did correct,[2] and the testimony of the poet himself, justify us in accepting it as a genuine sample of the writing of the Hawkshead days, at least until some proof to the contrary is adduced. Such proof M. Legouis finds in the fact that the style of these verses differs very much from that of the early poems of which we possess the original text. Any conclusions concerning Wordsworth's youthful tendencies drawn from the latter are flatly contradicted by the former. It is reasonable to deduce the characteristics of his early work from the only authentic examples of it, and then to question the authenticity of those which do not possess these characteristics. It seems the more reasonable in this case because the doubtful poems first appear in print long after they purport to have been written. Yet there is a plausible explanation of the difficulty.

The 'genuine samples' upon which M. Legouis bases his very able and discriminating study of Wordsworth's youthful style are indeed marked by an awkwardness in the use of language, and a love of morbid conceits and curiously elaborate phraseology. These are in noticeable contrast to the easy manipulation of language and metre, and the

---

[1] Among other things it would be necessary to prove that Wordsworth ever succeeds in changing the essential style of a poem by his numerous small alterations. *Peter Bell* has all the characteristics of a lyrical ballad, though it was not published until 1819; from the much corrected versions of *The Thorn* and *Simon Lee*, we can still deduce in the final edition most of the characteristics of the style of 1798.

[2] There are only two slight changes. In 1827 the line, 'Is up and cropping yet his later meal,' is altered to 'Is cropping audibly his later meal,' and *'comes* to heal' is substituted for *'seems* to heal.'

simplicity of thought and feeling in the *Extract* and the *Sonnet*. But these latter poems seem to be productions of Wordsworth's school-days at Hawkshead, while the earliest date for the other poems is 1787, the year Wordsworth entered the university. Of these poems, the *Sonnet on seeing Miss Helen Maria Williams weep*,[1] published March, 1787, while curiously exaggerated in thought, shows less departure from grammar and good usage than *An Evening Walk* and the *Descriptive Sketches;* and, of these two, the later and more powerful poem is also the most faulty with respect to style. Hence, for a time, Wordsworth's sins seem to increase with his increase in vigor and originality.

But, as we learn from the *Prelude*,[2]

> that first poetic faculty
> Of plain Imagination and severe

was greatly impaired by the influx of new and alien experiences between the time that Wordsworth left, or was preparing to leave, his own native hills for the busy world, and the time when he returned to them, and found peace of mind, and the lost simplicity of life and style, among the associations of his boyhood. This unwholesome period of his life seems to correspond with the dates of the poems on which M. Legouis bases his study of Wordsworth's early style (1787-1794). It is distinguished from his vigorous and healthy childhood by the same marks that distinguish the verse written at this time from the productions which we have taken to represent the work of his school-days.

---

[1] Of course it is not absolutely certain that Wordsworth wrote this poem. The reasons for attributing it to him are well stated by Professor Harper (*William Wordsworth* 1. 148-149). Since the authorship is uncertain, I do not think it can furnish much evidence concerning Wordsworth's early style.

[2] *Prelude* 12. 89-147.

On the one hand, there is the loss of the simplicity and unity of imaginative feeling associated with his delight in external nature, and his unquestioning acceptance of the only type of experience that he knew. The adaptation to a new environment and to a new world of ideas meant a temporary disorganizing of his whole intellectual life, and the growth of a self-conscious and analytic habit of mind, which also showed itself in a disorganization of an earlier and simpler style.

On the other hand, there is a distinct increase in intellectual power. From his graceful school-boy work we should derive very little notion of the real magnitude and strength of Wordsworth's genius. He seems to be only another disciple of the *Il Penseroso* landscape-school of Collins, Warton, and Bowles, with a distinct vein of his own, perhaps, and occasional felicity of melody or phrase, but not essentially different or more powerful. With the *Descriptive Sketches* it is otherwise. 'Seldom, if ever,' wrote Coleridge,[1] 'was the emergence of an original poetic genius above the literary horizon more evidently announced. In the form, style, and manner of the whole poem, and in the structure of the particular lines and periods, there is a harshness and acerbity connected and combined with words and images all aglow, which might recall those products of the vegetable world, where gorgeous blossoms rise out of the hard and thorny rind and shell, within which the rich fruit was elaborating. The language was not only peculiar and strong, but at times knotty and contorted, as by its own impatient strength; while the novelty and struggling crowds of images, acting in conjunction with the difficulties of the style, demanded always a greater closeness of attention, than poetry, (at all events than descriptive poetry) has a right to claim.'

This correspondence of the known dates of one group of early poems with a period of unrest and unequal develop-

[1] *B. L.* 1. 56.

ment of new energies, described in the *Prelude,* explains the immense difference between this verse and that which seems to have been produced before his disturbing sally into the world beyond his northern hills. 'The poetic Psyche,' says Coleridge,[1] 'in its process to full development, undergoes as many changes as its Greek name-sake, the butterfly.' It is not remarkable, therefore, that the young Wordsworth should have had more than one early style. His development in this respect is not unique. 'Perhaps a similar process has happened to others,' writes Coleridge,[2] 'but my earliest poems were marked by an ease and simplicity, which I have studied, perhaps with inferior success, to impress on my later compositions.' The words in which he describes his later efforts to prune the luxuriance and peculiarity of phrase which succeeded this earlier simplicity might be applied without change to Wordsworth's ineffectual attempts to alter the *Descriptive Sketches*[3]*:* 'In the after editions, I pruned the double epithets with no sparing hand, and used my best efforts to tame the swell and glitter both of thought and diction; though in truth, these parasite plants of youthful poetry had insinuated themselves into my longer poems with such intricacy of union, that I was often obliged to omit disentangling the weed, from the fear of snapping the flower.' The apologetic description of this unwholesome stage in a young poet's development prefixed by Keats to *Endymion* is well known: 'The imagination of a boy is healthy, and the mature imagination of a man is healthy; but there is a space of life between, in which the soul is in a ferment, the character undecided, the way of life uncertain, the ambition thick-sighted: thence proceeds mawkishness, and all the thousand bitters which those men I speak of must necessarily taste in going over the following pages.' It is in this space of life between boyhood and man-

---

[1] *B. L.* 1. 57.
[2] *Ibid.* 1. 4.
[3] *Ibid.* 1. 3.

hood that Wordsworth's early poems cease to be simple and clear.

Accordingly, before we turn to the more particular consideration of this second early style, we seem to be justified in summing up the results of our study of Wordsworth's earliest poems as follows: When, at fourteen, Wordsworth's discovery of his own power to produce the music of 'words in tuneful order' happened to coincide with the sudden recognition of the novelty of his own observations and adventures among his own hills, he was naturally led to write of these marvels. This caused him to turn away from the school of Pope, which could furnish him few models of such descriptive writing, to the landscape-school of the later part of the century, which derived so much of its inspiration from Milton's minor poems. Instead of the heroic couplet, he employs the octosyllabic verse of *Il Penseroso*, which was the mark of the school, and had been skilfully used by Collins, Dyer, and Warton. This inevitably led the clever and imitative boy to reproduce the easy and unfettered melody, the direct and simple expression, the clear natural imagery, and the general tone of pathos, which were characteristic of the reaction against Pope. The literary reminiscences in this verse all reflect reading of this type. The *Extract* is in the metre of *Il Penseroso*,[1] and in one case seems to reflect the plaintive Bowles.[2] The plaintiveness of Bowles, however, is so seldom original in its expression that almost anything apparently borrowed from him might have been borrowed from his masters. The sonnet is variously suggestive of

[1] This metre was also a favorite with Lady Winchelsea, who gave it some of the music of Marvel's tetrameters.
[2] 7-8. Cf. Bowles, Sonnet XV, 10-11. Of course, since the first sonnets of Bowles did not appear until 1789, lines borrowed from Bowles must have been added later. I do not deny the possibility of such corrections and additions; I merely believe that in this case, as in his later poems, Wordsworth did not succeed in altering the essential character and style of the verse.

Cowper,[1] Lady Winchelsea,[2] and Bowles. A later recurrence to the same style, in the *Lines written on the Thames* in 1789, is frankly imitative of Collins. This reveals the source of the simplicity. It is not the simplicity of Wordsworth's later style, transferred thither by a judicious correcting hand. It is as clearly the result of imitation as the more oratorical and conventional ease of the *School Exercise* in the manner of Pope.

But the poetic development of these years cannot be measured by the finished achievements alone. Much of the verse composed at Hawkshead never saw the light in its original form; but it became the foundation of many of the poems of Wordsworth's later years. From this early time dates the substance of the *Lines left upon a Seat in a Yew-Tree,* and part of the expression. It is not usually recognized that these lines are a kind of preliminary sketch of the Solitary in the *Excursion;* and that one of Wordsworth's most mature and subtle studies of character has thus a certain basis in the writing and observation of his school-days. The *Prelude* may have a similar foundation in his first autobiographical effort—a 'long poem running on my own adventures, and the scenery of the country in which I was brought up,' and containing 'thoughts and images, most of which have been dispersed through my other writings.' Since Wordsworth paraphrases the conclusion of this poem for the *Prelude,* he may also have used descriptions of his 'adventures' in his curiously vivid reproduction of the fears and spiritual dramas of childhood. His account of the black crag that seemed to stride after him,[3]

---

[1] With the line, 'Calm is all Nature as a resting wheel,' cf. Cowper, *The Task* 1. 367 ff., and *Fragment* 14-17 by Lady Anne Winchelsea (*Poems* and *Extracts, chosen by Wordsworth,* pp. 13-14). See a similar figure in the sonnets beginning, *If these brief Records* 9-11. (*The Poetical Works of Wordsworth,* Oxford edition, p. 270.)

[2] *Wordsworthiana,* p. 330.

[3] *Prelude* 2. 357-400.

and of his impatient waiting on the windy height for the 'palfreys that should bear us home,'[1] suggest an experience consciously heightened by a youthful poet, and a superstitious compunction which originally may have had a more conventionally religious coloring.[2] Several youthful poems also seem to be reproduced in the eighth book of the *Prelude*,[3] in the lines ending with the paraphrase of *Dear native Regions*. If only he had preserved the original, describing the wet rock sparkling in the evening radiance like the burnished shield of some dead knight, or the glittering entrance to a fairy cave! It might have been an interesting contrast to some of the *Lyrical Ballads*.

Although the romantic substance of most of the verses did not please Wordsworth's mature taste, he himself declares that all of them had a basis in truthful observation—that his most airy fancies revolved around a substantial center. This is certainly true of the only specimens of his work at Hawkshead that he preserved. Imitations as they are, they are at the same time genuine expressions of unified knowledge and feeling; and hence they have a charm and an artistic completeness that are lacking in his more powerful *Descriptive Sketches*. The *Sonnet*, especially, does not suffer by its position in the edition of 1807, side by side with some of Wordsworth's finest efforts in this type of verse.[4] It is so clear-cut, so unique in its own felicity of observation and phrase, that it seems to preclude comparison with its more powerful neighbors. This charm

---

[1] *Ibid.* 12. 287-316.
[2] Note especially 314-316.
[3] *Prelude* 8. 365-475.
[4] Wordsworth himself says that, in his schooldays at Hawkshead, Fancy
> could feed at Nature's call
> Some pensive musings which might well beseem
> Maturer years.
> *Prelude* 8. 456-458.

of Wordsworth's juvenile efforts was recognized by the critic of the volumes of 1815,[1] who, in the tone of pious exhortation made fashionable by Jeffrey, remarks that they show what Wordsworth might have done, had he not been led astray by his lamentable theories. But Wordsworth had gone astray long before he gave any public expression to his theories. He was not born to stop with the development of sixteen, even if this did make him a pensive landscape-poet of the first order. The energy so characteristic of his childhood had to shape for itself new and greater forms, even at the expense of harshness, and crudity, and failure.

3. *The Cambridge Period.*

Between 1787 and 1793 Wordsworth's boyish interest in the poetic expression of what was novel and wonderful in his own experience took a more ambitious form.

> Those were the days
> Which also first emboldened me to trust
> With firmness, hitherto but slightly touched
> By such a daring thought, that I might leave
> Some monument behind me which pure hearts
> Should reverence. The instinctive humbleness,
> Maintained even by the very name and thought
> Of printed books and authorship, began
> To melt away; and further, the dread awe
> Of mighty names was softened down and seemed
> Approachable, admitting fellowship
> Of modest sympathy. Such aspect now,
> Though not familiarly, my mind put on,
> Content to observe, to achieve, and to enjoy.[2]

But with growing power came a temporary difficulty in the manipulation of language, which was in notable contrast with his earlier facility, and a wilfulness of fancy and con-

---

[1] *Monthly Review* 78. 233.
[2] *Prelude* 6. 52-65.

ceit, which was the result of a new self-consciousness, and of rapidly developing intellectual energies.

The difficulty with language Wordsworth himself ascribes partly to an inexperienced attempt to conform to 'book-notions and to rules of art,' and partly to the practice of composing Latin verse at school.[1]

> The dangerous craft of culling term and phrase
> From languages that want the living voice
> To carry meaning to the natural heart.

The first led him to incorporate into his own verse any word or phrase that had pleased him in his desultory reading, usually with some modification or exaggeration that was not always for the best. The second resulted in some eccentricities of grammar and syntax more suitable to a highly inflected language, with a variable order and a complex structure, than to an uninflected language like English, which is so largely dependent upon the order of words.

However, the book-notions and rules of art did not prevent Wordsworth from being catholic and enterprising in his choice of a vocabulary. He does not elevate his style, or confine himself to a certain type of words, or even indulge in refined periphrasis, in accordance with the traditions of the eighteenth century. He takes a good word wherever he finds it. Accordingly terms from the northern dialects—such as *gill*,[2] *intake*,[3] *sugh*,[4] etc.—stand side by side with unusual Latin forms borrowed from Milton. He is especially interested in words denoting color and sound. He speaks of the 'sullen dark-brown mere,'[5] of the 'tawny earth,'[6] 'pale-blue rocks,'[7] etc., seeking to differentiate color

[1] *Ibid.* 6. 110-112. Cf. *B. L.* I. 13.
[2] *E. W.* 72.
[3] *E. W.* 65.
[4] *E. W.* 317; *D. S.* 437.
[5] *E. W.* 371.
[6] *E. W.* 170.
[7] *E. W.* 149.

from color, and shade from shade, as well as the English language will permit. Similarly, he takes onomatopœic words expressing sound from every source—colloquial or literary. He speaks of the chisel's clinking sound.'[1] 'Each clanking mill, that broke the murmuring streams,'[2] 'The distant forge's swinging thump profound'[3]; and makes liberal use of the suggestions that he finds in the poetry of Gray or Milton—such as the phrase 'drowsy tinklings,'[4] the word 'complain'[5] as applied to the note of the owl, the 'droning flight' of the beetle,[6] and the curfew 'swinging low with sullen roar.'[7] The same desire to add to his vocabulary leads him to adopt any unusual epithet which he discovers in reading. Like Warton, he speaks of the 'embattled clouds.'[8] Like Cowper, and unlike his own later self, he finds the note of the owl 'boding.'[9] Where Milton had spoken of 'rocking winds,' he speaks of 'rocking shades'[10]; in imitation of the line, 'minute drops from off the eaves,' he creates the compound, 'minute-steps'[11]; the expression 'huddling brook' becomes 'huddling rill'[12]; 'dim religious light' is copied in the phrase 'dim religious groves,'[13] etc.

[1] *E. W.* 145.
[2] *D. S.* 766.
[3] *E. W.* 445.
[4] Gray, *Elegy* 8. *D. S.* 435, 508; *E. W.* 354; cf. *Waggoner* 1. 26. 'That far-off tinkling's drowsy cheer.'
[5] *E. W.* 443. Cf. *Elegy* 10.
[6] *E. W.* 314. A reminiscence of *Elegy* 7 and *Lycidas* 28 combined. Cf. a similar union of suggestions from Milton and Gray in the line (*E. W.* 315), 'The whistling swain that plods his ringing way.'
[7] *Il Penseroso* 76. Cf. *E. W.* 318: 'The solemn curfew swinging long and deep.'
[8] *E. W.* 55. Cf. Warton, *Pleasures of Melancholy* 294.
[9] *E. W.* 392. Cf. *The Task* 1. 205.
[10] *E. W.* 238. Cf. *Il Penseroso* 126.
[11] *Il Penseroso* 130.
[12] *E. W.* 71. Cf. *Comus* 496.
[13] *D. S.* 604. Cf. *Il Penseroso* 160.

This practice is well described by M. Legouis[1]: 'Lady Winchelsea said that children's tears are merely "April drops," but Wordsworth, speaking of his own childhood, writes,

> When Transport kissed away my April tear.

Thompson invoked inspiration from her "hermit seat," (*Summer* 15), but Wordsworth, to whom the epithet appears an ingenious one, boldly applies it to the wave of a solitary lake ("hermit waves"), or to the door of a humble Swiss cottage hidden among the mountains ("hermit doors"). . . . Whereas Gray spoke of the "cock's shrill clarion," Wordsworth speaks of his "clarion throat." Gray represented the Nile as brooding "o'er Egypt with his watery wing"; Wordsworth pictures the wave of Liberty as brooding "the nations o'er with Nile-like wings." . . . Pope calls the second son of William the Conqueror his "second hope"; Wordsworth describes the eldest son of a poor vagrant as her "elder grief." With Pope the repose of death is the "Sabbath of the tomb"; for Wordsworth the canton of Unterwalden, with its silent summits, is a "Sabbath region." But the occasions on which Wordsworth has borrowed are so numerous that a special edition would be required to exhaust the list. Suffice it to say that, besides the poets already mentioned, many others of the eighteenth century are laid under contribution by him, whether the fact is acknowledged in his notes, and by quotation marks, or not, such as Young, Home, Smollett, Beattie. To these might be added two French names, Delille and Rosset, the author of *L'Agriculture ou les Georgiques Françaises,* the most awkwardly periphrastic of our descriptive poets. Of course Wordsworth's imitations are not strictly limited to eighteenth century bards; some incrustations from Spenser, Shakespeare, and especially Milton, are to be discovered in his mosaic-work; he even makes use of passages from the

---

[1] *The Early Life of William Wordsworth,* p. 140 ff.

Bible, which look very strange in the form of his elaborate couplet. To contemporary poets he seems to owe very little; only a Scotch word to Burns, whom he names, a touch to Langhorne, more perhaps to Cowper's *Task*, and most to Samuel Rogers' *Pleasures of Memory*, of which he makes no mention.'

Not only does he make use of all words and phrases that he can acquire in reading; he also attempts to widen the application of familiar words by a daring metaphorical use:—'He *tastes* the meanest note that swells the gale.'[1]

>   the crashing wood
> Gives way, and half its pines *torment* the flood.[2]

His compounds are equally bold: 'lip-dewing Song,'[3] 'ringlet-tossing Dance,'[4] 'oar-forgotten floods,'[5] day-deserted home,'[6] etc.

Many of these expressions are exaggerated enough, as Wordsworth soon discovered; but the imaginative enterprise that they display is remarkable. This is not the remnant of an old style; it is the crude but vigorous beginning of the new. To say that these poems are in the 'poetic diction' of the eighteenth century is to speak, apparently, without having undergone the sad experience of reading the miscellanies of that period. Wordsworth does not juggle the old familiar expressions—'balmy zephyrs,' 'blushing Flora,' 'paint the dewy meads,' etc.—into a slightly different position, and imagine he has made a new poem. He finds a new expression for a new image—even at the cost of being ridiculous; and in this lay the hope and the beginning of a new poetry.

[1] *D. S.* 20.
[2] *D. S.* 212.
[3] *D. S.* 99.
[4] *D. S.* 99.
[5] *D. S.* 135.
[6] *D. S.* 167.

But it is in syntax, rather than in vocabulary, that Wordsworth is most original. His peculiarities in this respect are enumerated by M. Legouis: 'We find archaisms in the forms of certain verbs[1]; verbs now neuter employed in an archaic sense as active[2]; irregular suppression of the article[3]; violent suppression of an auxiliary,[4] or of a verb[5]; employment of obsolete words,[6] or of words

[1] As examples of such archaisms, M. Legouis cites the use of *forgot* for *forgotten,* *broke* for *broken,* *ope* for *open,* etc. Strictly speaking, these could hardly be called archaic forms in Wordsworth's time; both forms had existed side by side in poetry from the first, and had been used interchangeably by representative writers like Shakespeare, Milton, Pope, and Cowper. Indeed *broke* seems actually to be a later form than *broken* (see *N. E. D.*), and *forgot* is the favorite form in Milton, Pope, and Cowper. Since Wordsworth rejected the forms *ope* and *broke* (as a past participle) in all his poetry written after 1797, we may assume that he felt these forms to be, if not archaic, at least merely poetic. But this is not true of *forgot* (as a past participle), which he continues to use to the end.

[2] M. Legouis cites as examples the use of *gaze* for *gaze on* (E. W. 17-18, 57, 130), and *to listen* for *listen to* (E. W. 436). In these forms, Wordsworth is following the usage of Milton, as opposed to that of earlier poets like Shakespeare and Spenser (cf. *P. L.* 8. 258, *P. R.* 1. 414, *Comus* 551. The transitive use of *gaze* seems to be later than the intransitive form (see *N. E. D.*). M. Legouis adds: 'Observe also the strained use, in an active sense, of *to course* (*E. W.* 31), *to roam* (*E. W.* 219), *to rove* (*D. S.* 80).'

[3] As examples M. Legouis cites *E. W.* 121, 446; *D. S.* 228.

[4] As an example M. Legouis cites *E. W.* 226. Cf. *Lines left upon a Seat in a Yew-tree* 4. 'What if these barren boughs the bee not loves.'

[5] The example given by M. Legouis, 'Spur-clad his nervous feet, and firm his tread' (*E. W.* 131) may not be felt by most English readers to be unusual. It is a construction common, not only in verse, but even in prose, though the usual order in prose would be 'his nervous feet spur-clad,' etc.

[6] M. Legouis cites *illume,* for *illumine.* as an example of such obsolete words. Like some of the other forms which M. Legouis calls archaic, *illume* is not a survival of an earlier word, but was a poetic form from the first, introduced later than the word which

used in an obsolete sense, at times with a somewhat pedantic regard for etymology,[1] or of words exceedingly rare,[2] if not newly coined[3]; abnormal constructions, for instance, the imitation of the ablative absolute, to which Milton was very partial[4]; misuse of the inversion which consists in making the subject follow the verb, by employing it without beginning the sentence with any of the adverbs that justify its use[5]; separation of relative and antecedent for the sake of elegance[6]; nouns in oblique cases placed before those

M. Legouis believes to be its modern representative. 'A poetical shortening of illumine,' says the *N. E. D.* Like other poetic forms, this was later abandoned by Wordsworth. Outside of the poems of 1793, there is but one example of its use—in the line 'An aspect tenderly illumined,' in the poem beginning 'Departing summer,' Oxford edition, p. 498.

[1] M. Legouis cites, as examples, *ruining* for *falling down* (D. S. 203), *haply* for *perhaps* (D. S. 410), *hapless* for *unhappy* (E. W. 239), *aspires* for *ascends* (D. S. 732). The use of *ruining* is probably a reminiscence of *P. L.* 6. 868. Of *haply* the *N. E. D.* says, 'Now archaic or poetic.' But the word *hapless* is not so designated; it is not infrequent in modern prose.

[2] As examples M. Legouis cites *viewless* for *invisible* (E. W. 148; D. S. 36, 92, 227, 548, 648); *moveless* for *motionless* (E. W. 104, 206, D. S. 226, etc.); *sombrous* for *dark* (E. W. 72). *Viewless* and *moveless* are words to which Dorothy Wordsworth especially objected in her criticisms of the poems of 1793 (L. W. F. 1. 50). *Viewless* immediately suggests Shakespeare's line, 'To be imprisoned in the viewless winds' (*Meas. for Meas.* 3. 1. 124). It also occurs in the poetry of Milton (*P. L.* 3. 518; *Comus* 92, etc.). The citations in the *N. E. D.* illustrating the use of *sombrous* do not suggest that it is an obsolete word, or a word confined to verse. In Wordsworth's poetry it is used only in the *Evening Walk*.

[3] As examples, M. Legouis cites *unbreathing* (D. S. 787), and *unpathway'd* for *pathless* (D. S. 285).

[4] E. W. 145. For the use of the ablative absolute in English, see Ross, 'The Absolute Participle in Middle and Modern English,' *Pub. Mod. Lang. Ass.* 8. 245 ff.

[5] M. Legouis cites E. W. 44, 70, 123, 230, 280, 365, 377, 428; D. S. 18, 62, 65, 146-147, 217, 229, 287, 555, 566, 701.

[6] E. W. 189.

which govern them, a construction which Wordsworth manages with especial awkwardness, and never entirely discards[1]; violent displacement of the direct complement, which is too short for the purpose, to make it precede the verb[2]; inversion of the direct pronominal object, with all the characteristics of one of Milton's Latin constructions,[3] various uncommon elliptical constructions,[4] or odd inversions of different kinds[5]; adjectives arbitrarily made to do duty as adverbs[6]; substantives used as adjectives[7]; and compound words either very rare or of the poet's own invention.[8]

This curious style may be illustrated by the following passage[9]:

>   An idle voice the sabbath region fills
>   Of Deep that calls to Deep across the hills,
>   Broke only by the melancholy sound
>   Of drowsy bells for ever tinkling round;
>   Faint wail of eagle melting into blue
>   Beneath the cliffs, and pine-woods steady sugh;
>   The solitary heifer's deepen'd low;
>   Or rumbling heard remote of falling snow.

[1] *E. W.* 321, *D. S.* 268, 390-391, 502.
[2] *D. S.* 122, 255.
[3] *D. S.* 45-47.
[4] *E. W.* 94-95.
[5] *D. S.* 11-12, 794.
[6] *E. W.* 149, *D. S.* 377. Cf. Wordsworth's objection to *fruitless* for *fruitlessly*—Appendix on Poetic Diction.
[7] *E. W.* 137, 153; *D. S.* 177, 299, 432, 558, 581, 697, 718, 720, 775, cited by M. Legouis. Cf. Wordsworth's later objection to this habit (Oxford edition, p. viii).
[8] Cf. *The Early Life of William Wordsworth*, p. 135, foot note: 'Every writer, whether of prose or of poetry, has a right to form new compound words, and it is needless to point out any but those which are somewhat obscure, or demand some investigation if they are to be understood. For example; '*hotlow-parting* oar,' i. e. forming a hollow in the water as well as dividing it (*E. W.* 439); '*hollow-blustering coast*,' i. e. sounding hollow beneath the sudden squall. Thomson had applied the same epithet to the mind (*Winter* 987).'
[9] *D. S.* 432-445.

> Save that, the stranger seen below, the boy
> Shouts from the echoing hills with savage joy.
> When warm from myrtle bays and tranquil seas,
> Comes on, to whisper hope, the vernal breeze,
> When hums the mountain bee in May's glad ear,
> And emerald isles to spot the heights appear.

Here, as may be seen at once, the fault lies, not in the choice of words, but in the syntax. The young poet is trying to employ in English the less restricted order of Latin verse. The awkward use of the participle in lines 434, 439, and 440 of this passage; the separation of a word from its modifier in lines 432 and 433; and the placing of the verb before the subject, and the adverbial phrase before the verb which it completes, in lines 444 and 445—these are all the result of disregarding the familiar conventions of the spoken English sentence, on which the intelligibility of our uninflected speech is so largely dependent. Most of them may be paralleled in the poetry of Milton, from whom, indeed, a very large number of peculiar words and forms in these poems are directly borrowed. Milton, rather than the landscape-school which M. Legouis assigns as the model of these poems, seems to be directly responsible for most of the vagaries of language in them. Despite Wordsworth's obvious indebtedness to his predecessors in the latter part of the eighteenth century, neither the faults nor the virtues of these descriptive poems are really representative of the type of poetic diction prevalent before him. As we have pointed out, the best achievement of the eighteenth century was a clear and natural order and syntax; its worst achievement was a set of periphrastic phrases, which did duty for simple words and original observations. Neither of these are characteristic of Wordsworth's Cambridge poems. A comparison of the verses already given as a specimen of the 'gaudiness and inane phraseology' of Wordsworth's time with the passage from the *Descriptive Sketches* just quoted will establish the truth of this statement. The former is as superior in grammatical clearness and metrical ease as it is inferior in freshness and originality of substance and phrase. As far as the landscape-poets escaped from the style of the Augustan age, they attained to the clean-cut, though, for the most part, unambitious imagery, the sincere but gentle imaginative feeling, and the quiet melody, that are more characteristic of Wordsworth's school-boy work than of the *Descriptive Sketches,* which Coleridge likened to some gorgeous and knotty tropical growth. But, save for an occasional liberty borrowed from Milton or Spenser, the landscape-poets tended to preserve the grammatical structure which Dryden and his age had succeeded in establishing.

Perhaps the use of absolute constructions in Pope's translation of Homer, or Young's *Night Thoughts,* or the poetry of Thomson and Bowles, or a lapse from 'correctness' in the descriptive verse of Dyer, had encouraged Wordsworth in his reproduction of Milton's eccentricities; but, for the most part, he seems to go back to the great original of these faults, and to copy him directly. As an example of this Miltonic influence, we may cite the use of *gaze*[1] and *listen*[2] as transitive verbs, contrary to the usage of Spenser and Shakespeare; of *ruin* as an intransitive verb—

> And, *ruining* from the cliffs, their deafening load
> Tumbles,[3]

with which we may compare Milton's line,

>   Hell saw
> Heaven *ruining* from Heaven[4];

the quasi-adverbial use of *remote* in the line, 'Or rumbling heard remote of falling snow,'[5] which echoes the lines in *Paradise Lost:*

[1] *E. W.* 57, 130; *D. S.* 556-557.
[2] *E. W.* 436.
[3] *D. S.* 203.
[4] *P. L.* 6. 868.
[5] *D. S.* 439.

> Their rising all at once was as the sound
> Of thunder heard remote[1];

the frequent use of the phrase, 'bosom'd deep,'[2] in imitation of Milton's 'bosom'd high in tufted trees,' etc.[3]

Although the influence of Milton, and the practice of writing in Latin, seem to be responsible for the mannerisms of the descriptive poems, this early difficulty with syntax is characteristic of Wordsworth. It is due to the same tendency that makes his critical utterances obscure—the tendency of his intellectual ideas to become involved with intense emotional and imaginative associations, which his readers do not always share. Sometimes, in his later blank verse, it was as difficult for Wordsworth to go straight to the point in a sentence as it was for him to go straight to the climax in a narrative. The thought was sufficiently clear and energetic; it did not lose sight of the final goal; but it carried so much weight that the movement was somewhat impeded. It is necessary to recognize this difficulty in making use of the clear but limited sentence-structure of the eighteenth century, when it first appears in Wordsworth's poetry, because it explains some of his later experiments. Dryden and his followers had rendered an essential service, by making the written language correspond more nearly to the structure of the spoken language; but their syntax was too impassioned, too inexpressive, for Wordsworth's freer and bolder genius. He needed a more flexible instrument, and, in the end, he found it.

But if Wordworth's syntax is peculiar, his figures of speech are more so. 'Instances of personification, which in Collins and Gray are already plentiful, swarm in the *Evening Walk* and the *Descriptive Sketches*. *Impatience,* "panting upward," climbs mountains[4]; obsequious *Grace* pursues

---

[1] *P. L.* 2. 477.
[2] *E. W.* 13; *D. S.* 81; cf. *L'Allegro* 78.
[3] The use of *erroneous, D. S.* 689, suggests Milton, *P. L.* 7. 20.
[4] *E. W.* 35.

the male swan on the lake, while *tender Cares* and *domestic Loves* swim in pursuit of the female[1]; *Pain* has a sad family[2]; *Independence* is the child of *Disdain*[3]; *Hope* leans ceaselessly on *Pleasure's* funereal urn[4]; *Consumption*, "with cheeks o'erspread by smiles of baleful glow," passes through the villages of France on a pale horse[5]; "*Oppression* builds her thick-ribb'd tow'rs"; *Machination* flees "panting to the centre of her mines"; *Persecution* decks her bed (of torture) with ghastly smiles; *Ambition* piles up mountains, etc.[6] . . . The poet's fancy becomes still more whimsical when he attributes human or animal characteristics, not to abstractions which he can endow with any form he pleases, but to objects or phenomena so familiar to us that our knowledge of their nature protests against such a travesty. The blood which flows from the wounded feet of the chamois-hunter is "Lapp'd by the panting *tongue* of thirsty skies."[7] The mountain-shadow creeps toward the crest of the hill "with *tortoise foot*."[8] "Silent stands th' admiring *vale*" (i. e. the villagers).[9] Frequently false pathos is mingled with these effects. An old man's lyre is itself not old, but *aged*.[10] The Grand Chartreuse, hoary with snow, *weeps* "beneath his chill of mountain gloom."[11] And these constantly recurring personifications extend even to the grammar. The neuter gender tends to disappear,[12] and

---

[1] *E. W.* 200, 206-207.
[2] *D. S.* 2 (taken from Pope, *Essay on Man* 2. 110).
[3] *D. S.* 323-324.
[4] *D. S.* 518.
[5] *D. S.* 788-791.
[6] *D. S.* 792-804.
[7] *D. S.* 397.
[8] *D. S.* 105.
[9] *E. W.* 188.
[10] *D. S.* 171.
[11] *D. S.* 54.
[12] *Beacon* (*E. W.* 189); *steep* (*E. W.* 156); *mountain* (*E. W.* 336-339), etc., are masculine.

the genitive case,[1] commonly used only in reference to living beings, is curiously applied to words of every sort.'

This attempt to present everything by an image M. Legouis ascribes to the influence of Darwin. This may be true; but it is doubtful whether the passage in the *Biographia Literaria* on which M. Legouis bases this conclusion can refer to Wordsworth. Coleridge is speaking of admirers of Darwin with whom he used to dispute in his early Cambridge days.[2] At this time he did not know Wordsworth; and when the two young men met, Wordsworth had already recovered from any infatuation for verse of the type of the *Botanic Garden*—if he ever felt it. Besides, in the note to the *Descriptive Sketches,* which is his only critical utterance before the time of the *Lyrical Ballads,* he protests against Darwin's favorite term, *picturesque,* with considerable energy.

But whether Wordsworth is influenced by Darwin or not, his personifications are very different from most contemporary figures of this sort, including those of the *Botanic Garden.* To find anything really parallel to them we must go back to the metaphysical poets. As Coleridge noticed, the chief difficulty with the personifications of the eighteenth century is that they remain abstractions. The only sign of the supposed humanity (or divinity in the shape of humanity) of all these figures—Floras, Cynthias, Hopes, and Loves—of the period is the conventional symbol of the capital letter and some equally conventional adjective—*pale* Cynthia, *blushing* Flora, etc. Though Darwin makes a special effort to give human personalities to all his vegetable lovers, he does so mainly by a more liberal

---

[1] *E. W.* 76, 51; *D. S.* 274, 153, 225. Wordsworth never did share Coleridge's objection to this use of the genitive. See the many awkward examples of it under with words like *edge* ('lake's edge,' etc.) in the *Concordance.*

[2] *B. L.* I. 12.

use of general periphrastic terms, rather than by clearly individualizing the image:

> How the young rose, in *beauty's damask pride*,
> Drinks the warm blushes of his bashful bride.[1]

With Wordsworth it is quite different. In the first place, his personifications are distinguished from similar figures in most contemporary verse by the fact that he gives abstractions and inanimate things the personalities of the lower animals, rather than of divine beings. Peace is a redbreast[2]; Hope is a lark[3]; Reason may be a dog[4]; the evening shadows come down the vale on the wings of Beattie's owl[5]; etc. No doubt he felt better acquainted with animals than with 'heavenly maids.' The result of this is sometimes rather strange; but it is certainly a sign of the almost unconscious originality of the youthful poet. Moreover, he realizes his images intensely, even at the risk of being somewhat ridiculous. He is not content to speak vaguely of 'pale Cynthia.' When the image of the pale lady is suggested to his mind, it immediately becomes a separate and living entity. For example, he writes of the moon:

> By the deep quiet gloom appall'd, she sighs,
> Stoops her sick head, and shuts her weary eyes.[6]

Though the propriety of the image may certainly be questioned, there is no doubt that 'pale Cynthia' is a distinct person in the poet's imagination. Sometimes the reference

---

[1] Darwin, *Loves of the Plants* I. 17-18.
[2] *D. S.* 169.
[3] *D. S.* 632.
[4] *D. S.* 56.
[5] *E. W.* 191-192. Cf. the stanza quoted from Beattie's poem, *Retirement*, in *A Cento made by Wordsworth* (Oxford edition, p. 626).
[6] *D. S.* 221-222.

to the lady is more happy—as in that beautiful passage from the *Evening Walk,* which may be quoted in full, because in it are concentrated many of the finest characteristics of these poems:

>The bird, with fading light who ceas'd to thread
>Silent the hedge or steaming rivulet's bed,
>From his grey re-appearing tower shall soon
>Salute with boding note the rising moon,
>Frosting with hoary light the pearly ground,
>And pouring deeper blue to Æther's bound;
>Rejoic'd her solemn pomp of clouds to fold
>In robes of azure, fleecy white, and gold,
>While rose and poppy, as the glow-worm fades,
>Checquer with paler red the thicket shades.
>Now o'er the eastern hills, where Darkness broods
>O'er all its vanish'd dells, and lawns, and woods
>Where but a mass of shade the sight can trace,
>*She lifts in silence up her lovely face;*
>Above the gloomy valley flings her light,
>Far to the western slopes with hamlets white;
>And gives, where woods the checquer'd upland strew,
>To the green corn of summer autumn's hue.

But the artistic originality of this early work is not to be measured by its quaint exaggerations. In the passage just quoted (and this is thoroughly typical) there is something that at once explains the passionate enthusiasm with which Coleridge hailed the new genius. In the first place there is the accurate observation of the natural features, not as dead or static, but in their living and changing relations to each other—in the image of the grey re-appearing tower, the fading of the glow-worm, the appearance of the pale-red roses and poppies in the thicket, etc. His first poetic impulse had come to him when he noticed how the sunset radiance changed and glorified the familiar face of common things. The artistic motive thus suggested to him at fourteen is everywhere present in these early

[1] *E. W.* 389-406.

poems, not only in the subtle observations of the *Evening Walk,* but in the splendid climaxes of light and color in the *Descriptive Sketches.*

Perhaps it was this same experience that first stimulated Wordsworth's special interest in color, characteristic of the time when he was

> Bent over much on superficial things,
> Pampering myself with meagre novelties
> Of color and proportion.

Later, as Miss Pratt says of Wordsworth's mature poetry,[1] 'in contrast with the voice of wind and stream, forms and colors were to him external qualities, Nature's dress rather than the utterance of her life; and for this reason, though they appealed to Wordsworth's eye and were mingled with happy memories, they meant less and less to him as his mind became more mature and more watchful for 'the latent qualities and essences of things."'

This is true; but it becomes still more significant when we note, as Miss Pratt has failed to do,[2] the remarkable splendor and variety of color in these poems, whose lavishness in this respect can be paralleled only in the early work of Keats. Purity and self-restraint are the more notable where the energies are warm and powerful; and Wordsworth's later preference for the quiet green tints of field and wood is the more interesting when we perceive how his early poems flame with scarlet and gold—how he loves the light and fire of the setting sun more than all the secret and shadowy beauties of nature.

[1] *Color in English Romantic Poetry,* pp. 55-56.
[2] She notes that the early poems of Wordsworth employ color as lavishly as do the early poems of Keats (p. 57), who 'in wealth of color stands without a peer' (p. 88); but she fails to note the effectiveness and the originality of the color. The color of the young Wordsworth is imaginative, where that of the young Keats is merely decorative.

This interest in color is paralleled by an interest in sound—visible not only in successful attempts to differentiate the various notes and voices, but in an effort to make the sound an echo to the sense. In later years, although Wordsworth always tried to give melody and harmony to his verse, and was almost painfully conscious of an unpleasant jarring of sounds, he was not inclined to use the device of *onomatopœia*. In these early poems, however, there are many interesting examples of it. One of the most original of these is the line: 'Glad in their airy baskets, hang and sing'[1]; but there are many more obvious efforts:—

> the silver'd kite
> In many a *whistling circle wheels* her flight.[2]
> With pensive step to *measure my slow way*.[3]
> Sound of *clos'd gate* across the water borne.[4]
> *Hurrying the feeding hare through rustling corn.*[5]
> The distant forge's swinging thump profound.[6]

To achieve such effects in the metre of the heroic couplet was something of a triumph. Like everything else in the poems, they are not so much an imitation of an old form as the promise of a new, and point to the emergence above the horizon, not only of a new and vital genius, but of a very self-conscious artist.

4. *Study and Self-Criticism.*

No sooner had these efforts appeared than Wordsworth began to see their defects. In this he was greatly assisted by the candor of his family—not only of Dorothy, but of Christopher—then an undergraduate at Cambridge, who

[1] *E. W.* 150.
[2] *E. W.* 90.
[3] *D. S.* 165.
[4] *E. W.* 441.
[5] *E. W.* 442.
[6] *E. W.* 445.

here exercises for the first and last time, a vital influence on his brother's work. Dorothy and 'Kit' went through the poem, analyzing it line by line, and embodying their opinions in a bulky criticism which Christopher withheld until he could add the remarks of a friend at Cambridge.[1] This friend was very likely Coleridge. He and Christopher belonged to the same literary society, which discussed William's poems among other things; and in Christopher's diary he is the one member of the society whose opinions are especially quoted.[2]

Christopher also seems to have noticed the criticism of his brother's verse in the *Monthly Review*.[3] The Monthly Reviewer was a stupid person, who probably did not take the trouble to read the poems through; but he made one remark which seems to have sunk deep into Wordsworth's consciousness. He advised him and every other young maker of verses to look at his own thoughts until he was sure he understood them. No one could be a poet until 'his mind is strong enough to sustain this labor.' Long afterward Wordsworth gave to young William Rowan Hamilton the advice which he himself had received from this otherwise rather undiscerning critic.[4]

As a result of all these candid opinions, Wordsworth at once set to work to alter the poems. In 1794 he writes to Mathews that he has been correcting and adding to the verse published the preceding year, and remarks that he is sorry that he huddled the pieces into the world in so imperfect a form. 'But as I had done nothing by which to dis-

---

[1] *L. W. F.* 1. 51-52.
[2] *Social Life at the English Universities in the Eighteenth Century*. See the reprint of Christopher's diary in the Appendix.
[3] *Monthly Review* 12. 216-218.
[4] *L. W. F.* 2. 313. After analyzing Hamilton's verses as the critic in the *Monthly Review* had analyzed the *Descriptive Sketches*, Wordsworth remarks: 'The logical faculty has infinitely more to do with poetry than the young and inexperienced, whether writer or critic, ever dreams of.'

tinguish myself at the university,' he says,[1] 'I thought these little things might show that I could do something. They have been treated with unmerited contempt by some of the periodical publications, and others have spoken of them in higher terms than they deserve.'

According to Wordsworth's own statement, the result of these corrections is embodied in the version printed in 1820. Because of the poet's tendency to be a little inaccurate with regard to dates, and to keep retouching all his work even while it was going through the press, it is the custom to doubt his word in such matters. But it happens that the faults corrected in the version of 1820 are exactly the faults which he carefully avoids in his next effort—*Guilt and Sorrow;* and for the original form of this latter poem we have the testimony of Coleridge. Hence we seem to be justified in accepting Wordsworth's own statement. In the version of 1820 the structure of the language is somewhat improved; a few objectionable words or forms (such as *gaze* used as a transitive verb) are omitted; and some excellent lines are added. But the really notable feature is the uncompromising ejection of almost everything in the nature of a personification. In the first seventy lines of the *Evening Walk*, for instance, *Mirth, Memory*, soft *Affection*, and *Quiet* all disappear. Sometimes several lines are forced to disappear with them. Sometimes the change is more easily effected. Instead of 'soft Affection's ear' Wordsworth merely says 'unreluctant ear'; for the line 'Then Quiet led me up the huddling rill,' he writes 'Then, while I wandered up the huddling rill,' etc.

But while he was thus improving his technique, Wordsworth was also developing a theory of fine art. To the *Monthly Miscellany*, which he and Mathews were planning to edit, he was willing to contribute 'critical remarks upon Poetry, etc., etc.; upon the arts of Painting, Gardening, and

---

[1] *L. W. F.* 1. 67.

other subjects of amusement.'[1] If only these remarks had been written! We have almost no means of knowing what the substance of them would have been. Wordsworth's few early letters are notably lacking in literary criticism. All that is known is that he read John Scott of Amwell, whose emphasis upon clear and distinct imagery and desire to enrich poetry with new rural images must have coincided with Wordsworth's own boyish ambition. Besides the reference to Scott in the notes to the *Evening Walk*,[2] there is only one other indication that Wordsworth had been reflecting on the nature of fine art. In a note to the *Descriptive Sketches* he makes an emphatic protest against the Darwinian theory that poetry is painting in words, of which M. Legouis seems to consider him an adherent at this time: 'I had once given to these sketches the title of Picturesque; but the Alps are insulted in applying to them that term. Whoever, in attempting to describe their sublime features, should confine himself to the cold rules of painting would give his reader but a very imperfect idea of those emotions which they have the irresistible power of communicating to the most impassive imaginations. The fact is, that controuling influence, which distinguishes the Alps from all other scenery, is derived from images which disdain the pencil. Had I wished to make a picture of this scene I had thrown much less light into it. But I consulted nature and my own feelings. The ideas excited by the stormy sunset I am here describing owe their sublimity to that deluge of light, or rather of fire, in which nature had wrapped the immense forms around me; any intrusion of shade, by destroying the unity of the impression, had necessarily diminished its grandeur.'[3]

Perhaps this is the beginning of the theory of imagination which he and Coleridge later developed together. He

[1] *L. W. F.* 1. 66.
[2] Oxford edition, p. 595.
[3] *Ibid.* p. 608.

had already begun to assert the right and power of the imagination to modify and combine visual images in accordance with the dictates of impassioned feeling.

But, whatever Wordsworth's theories may have been at this time, the result of all this critical effort is visible in his next poem, which may best be described in Coleridge's glowing words[1]: 'I was in my twenty-fourth year, when I had the happiness of knowing Mr. Wordsworth personally, and while memory lasts, I shall hardly forget the sudden effect produced on my mind by his recitation of a manuscript poem, which still remains unpublished, but of which the stanza, and tone of the style, were the same as those of the "Female Vagrant," as originally printed in the first volume of the "Lyrical Ballads." There was here no mark of strained thought, or forced diction, no crowd or turbulence of imagery; and, as the poet hath himself well described in his lines "on revisiting the Wye," manly reflection, and human associations had given both variety and additional interest to natural objects, which in the passion and appetite of the first love they had seemed to him neither to need or permit. The occasional obscurities, which had arisen from an imperfect controul over the resources of his native language, had almost wholly disappeared, together with that worst defect of arbitrary and illogical phrases at once hackneyed and fantastic, which hold so distinguished a place in the *technique* of ordinary poetry, and will, more or less, alloy the earlier poems of the truest genius, unless the attention has been specifically directed to the worthlessness and incongruity. I did not perceive anything particular in the mere style of the poem alluded to during its recitation, except indeed such difference as was not separable from the thought and manner; and the Spenserian stanza, which always, more or less, recalls to the reader's mind Spenser's own style, would doubtless

---

[1] *B. L.* 1. 59.

have authorized, in my then opinion, a more frequent descent to the phrases of ordinary life, than could without an ill effect have been hazarded in the heroic couplet. It was not however the freedom from false taste, whether as to common defects, or to those more properly his own, which made so unusual an impression on my feelings immediately, and subsequently on my judgment. It was the union of deep feeling with profound thought; the fine balance of truth in observing with imaginative faculty in modifying the objects observed; and above all the original gift of spreading the tone, the *atmosphere,* and with it all the depth and height of the ideal world around forms, incidents, and situations, of which, for the common view, custom had bedimmed all the lustre, had dried up the sparkle and the dew drops.[1]

Thus, as early as 1796, Wordsworth had attained to an austere and imaginative simplicity of style. A slight awkwardness of language was still visible, but the extraneous and exaggerated ornaments were gone. As far as can be determined, this improvement was solely on the basis of reading confined, in the field of English literature, to the poets of the eighteenth century and the three great elder bards—Milton, Spenser, and Shakespeare. Apart from these, he had been especially interested in Italian and Latin poetry. During his Cambridge days he had read Ariosto and Tasso with such enthusiasm that, when he first went to France, his mind was more often preoccupied with thoughts of Erminia and Angelica than with the philosophical dialogues of Beaupuy.[2] In the years between the pub-

---

[1] The language is still a little unidiomatic. The inversions are numerous, as in 100, 159, 170, 185, 278, 330, 367, 547, etc. The article is frequently omitted, as in 99, 135, 136, 140, 142, 144, 187, etc. The auxiliary is omitted now and then, as in 3, 48, etc. There is also a large number of places in which a participle or noun in apposition is awkwardly used, as in 10, 66, 72, 148, etc.

[2] *Prelude* 9. 437-453. Concerning Wordsworth's Italian studies, see also *Memoirs* 1. 14.

lication of the descriptive poems and the meeting with Coleridge he had apparently turned back to the Latin authors, especially Horace and Juvenal. One of the passages added to the *Evening Walk*[1] is based on Horace; and the special literary enterprise of this period was a translation of Juvenal which he and Wrangham were making together.[2] Perhaps Mathews also took some interest in this; at least a copy of Juvenal was presented to Wordsworth by Mathews.[3] But of the special literary models of the *Lyrical Ballads*—the poetry of Chaucer, the *Reliques of Ancient Poetry*, and the literature before Dryden—we hear not a word. However, the source of this new influence at once becomes clear when we consider what Lamb and Coleridge had been doing up to this time.

[1] See the final version of the *Evening Walk*, 72-85 (Oxford edition, p. 3). This appears in the edition of 1820 as it is here written. It was probably one of those additions 'made shortly after publication' in 1793.
[2] *L. W. F.* I. 87-89, 92-98.
[3] This is now in the library of Mrs. Henry St. John, Ithaca, N. Y.

CHAPTER 4.

COLERIDGE AND HIS CIRCLE.

While Wordsworth was thus attaining to the practice of simplicity, Coleridge and Lamb had been developing the theory of it; and were religiously seeking out literary models of a style more pure and plain. The beginnings of this effort, which ended in the *Lyrical Ballads,* are to be found in the teaching of their doughty old schoolmaster at Christ's Hospital—the Rev. James Boyer.[1] 'He early moulded my taste to the preference of Demosthenes to Cicero, of Homer and Theocrites to Virgil, and again of Virgil to Ovid,' writes Coleridge.[2] 'He habituated me to compare Lucretius (in such extracts as I then read), Terence, and above all the chaster poems of Catullus, not only with the Roman poets of the, so called, silver and brazen ages; but with even those of the Augustan era; and on grounds of plain sense and universal logic to see and assert the superiority of the former in the truth and nativeness, both of their thoughts and diction. . . . In our own English compositions, (at least for the last three years of our school education,) he showed no mercy to phrase, metaphor, or image, unsupported by a sound sense, or where the same sense might have been conveyed with equal force and dignity in plainer words. Lute, harp, and lyre, Muse, Muses, and inspirations, Pegasus, Parnassus, and Hippocrene, were all an abomination to him. In fancy I can almost hear him now, exclaiming *"Harp? Harp? Lyre? Pen and ink, boy, you mean! Muse, boy, Muse?*

---

[1] 'Lamb speaks of himself as only a Deputy Grecian, and yet there is no doubt that he enjoyed the advantage of Boyer's tuition, even although that masterful instructor reserved his highest enthusiasm for Grecians absolute.'—Lucas, *The Life of Charles Lamb* 1. 74.

[2] *B. L.* 1. 4-5.

Your nurse's daughter, you mean! Pierian spring? Oh aye! the cloister-pump, I suppose!"'

Although for a time the youthful Coleridge neglected literature for philosophy, he did not forget the teaching of these early days. When the sonnets of Bowles appeared, he at once hailed them as models of simplicity and tenderness, and quite forgot the mysteries of Neoplatonism in his proselyting enthusisam for what seemed to him a new type of poetry.[1] As a matter of fact, Bowles was not very new. His verse alternately echoes Milton's minor poems and the sweeter cadences of Shakespeare—not to mention his master, Warton. But his pure and slender melodies fell gratefully upon the ear after the couplets of Pope and Erasmus Darwin.

Naturally Coleridge, with the conversational zeal for disseminating knowledge which marked him even then, enthusiastically recommended Bowles upon all occasions. In so doing he developed a whole theory of criticism, in which we already find dim intimations of the Preface to the *Lyrical Ballads.* The lively discussions begun then, and continued with renewed vigor after he met Wordsworth, are best described in his own words[2]: 'Among those with whom I conversed, there were, of course, very many who had formed their taste and their notions of poetry, from the writings of Pope and his followers; or to speak more generally, in that school of French poetry, condensed and invigorated by English understanding, which had predominated from the last century. I was not blind to the merits of this school, yet, as from inexperience of the world, and consequent want of sympathy with the general subjects of these poems, they gave me little pleasure, I doubtless undervalued the *kind,* and with the presumption of youth withheld from its masters the legitimate name of poets. I saw that the excellence of this kind consisted in

[1] *B. L.* 1. 7-10.
[2] *Ibid.* 1. 11-14.

just and acute observations on men and manners in an artificial state of society, as its matter and substance; and in the logic of wit, conveyed in smooth and strong epigrammatic couplets, as its *form*. Even when the subject was addressed to the fancy, or the intellect, as in the Rape of the Lock, or the Essay on Man; nay, when it was a consecutive narration, as in that astonishing product of matchless talent and ingenuity, Pope's translation of the Iliad; still a *point* was looked for at the end of each second line, and the whole was, as it were, a sorites, or, if I may exchange a logical for a grammatical metaphor, a *conjunction disjunctive,* of epigrams. Meantime the matter and diction seemed to me characterized not so much by poetic thoughts, as by thoughts *translated* into the language of poetry. On this last point, I had occasion to render my own thoughts gradually more and more plain to myself, by frequent amicable disputes concerning Darwin's *Botanic Garden,* which, for some years, was greatly extolled, not only by the *reading* public in general, but even by those, whose genius and natural robustness of understanding enabled them afterwards to act foremost in dissipating these "painted mists" that occasionally rise from the marshes at the foot of Parnassus. During my first Cambridge vacation, I assisted a friend in a contribution for a literary society in Devonshire: and in this I remember to have compared Darwin's work to the Russian palace of ice, glittering, cold, and transitory. In the same essay, too, I assigned sundry reasons, chiefly drawn from a comparison of passages in the Latin poets with the original Greek, from which they were borrowed, for the preference of Collins's odes to those of Gray; and of the simile in Shakespeare

> How like a younker or a prodigal,
> The scarfed bark puts from her native bay,
> Hugg'd and embraced by the strumpet wind!
> How like the prodigal doth she return,

> With over-weather'd ribs and ragged sails,
> Lean, rent, and beggar'd by the strumpet wind![1]

so the imitation in The Bard;

> Fair laughs the morn, and soft the zephyr blows
> While proudly riding o'er the azure realm
> In gallant trim the gilded vessel goes,
> Youth at the prow and PLEASURE at the helm;
> Regardless of the sweeping whirlwind's sway,
> That hush'd in grim repose, expects its evening prey.[2]

(in which, by the by, the words "realm" and "sway" are rhymes dearly purchased). I preferred the original on the ground, that in the imitation it depended wholly on the compositor's putting, or not putting, *a small Capital*, both in this, and in many other passages of the same poet, whether the words should be personifications, or mere abstractions. I mention this, because, in referring various lines in Gray to their original in Shakespeare and Milton, and in the clear perception how completely all the propriety was lost in the transfer; I was, at that early period, led to a conjecture, which, many years afterwards, was recalled to me from the same thought having been started in conversation, but far more ably, and developed more fully, by Mr. Wordsworth;—namely, that this style of poetry, which I have characterized above, as translations of prose thoughts into poetic language, had been kept up by, if it did not wholly arise from, the custom of writing Latin verses, and the great importance attached to these exercises in our public schools. Whatever might have been the case in the fifteenth century, when the use of the Latin tongue was so general among learned men, that Erasmus is said to have forgotten his native language; yet, in the present day it is not to be supposed that a youth can *think*

[1] *Merchant of Venice* 2. 6. 14-19.
[2] *The Bard* 70-75.

in Latin, or that he can have any other reliance on the force or fitness of his phrases, but the authority of the writer from whence he has adopted them.[1] Consequently he must first prepare his thoughts, and then pick out, from Virgil, Horace, Ovid, or perhaps more compendiously from his Gradus, halves and quarters of lines, in which to embody them.

'I never object to a certain degree of disputatiousness in a young man from the age of seventeen to that of four or five and twenty, provided I find him always arguing on one side of the question. The controversies, occasioned by my unfeigned zeal for the honor of a favorite contemporary, then known to me only by his works, were of great advantage, in the formation and establishment of my taste and critical opinions. In my defence of the lines running into each other, instead of closing at each couplet, and of natural language, neither bookish, nor vulgar, neither redolent of the lamp, nor of the kennel, such as *I will remember thee;* instead of the same thought tricked up in the rag-fair finery of,

> thy image on her wing
> Before my Fancy's eye shall Memory bring,

I had continually to adduce the metre and diction of the Greek poets from Homer to Theocritus inclusive; and still more of our elder English poets from Chaucer to Milton. Nor was this all. But as it was my constant reply to authorities brought against me from later poets of great name, that no authority could avail in opposition to *Truth, Nature, Logic,* and the *Laws of Universal Grammar;* actuated too by my former passion for metaphysical investigations; I labored at a solid foundation, in which permanently to ground my opinions, in the component faculties of the human mind itself, and their comparative dignity of importance.'

[1] Cf. *Prelude* 6. 105-115.

We might be tempted to think that Coleridge was transferring his later opinions to these earlier days were it not for an abundance of contemporary testimony concerning these enthusiastic conversations. 'Coleridge talked Greek,' remarks Christopher Wordsworth[1] (in describing a meeting at which 'Dr. Darwin, Miss Seward, Mrs. Smith, Bowles, and my Brother' were discussed), 'and spouted out of Bowles.' 'My poetical taste was much meliorated by Bowles,' writes Southey in 1795,[2] 'and the constant company of Coleridge,' who probably 'spouted out of Bowles' in Southey's presence also. But it is in the letters of Lamb to Coleridge, just before the close association between Wordsworth and Coleridge began, and in the new *Monthly Magazine*, for which this group of ambitious young poets were writing, that we find the clearest indications of the theories of the *Lyrical Ballads*.

'Cultivate simplicity, Coleridge,' is the burden of Lamb's letters. 'Banish elaborateness; for simplicity springs spontaneous from the heart and carries into daylight its own modest buds, and genuine, sweet, and clear flowers of expression. I allow no hot-beds in the garden of Parnassus.'[3] The simplicity which he so much admired in Bowles, Lamb found also in Burns and Cowper, and in the genuinely imaginative figures and personifications of 'our elder bards,' whom he wished Coleridge to strive to bring 'into more general fame.'[4] The simplicity he loves is not the elegant simplicity of Pope; it is naïve and quaint and homely. At one time he remarks, apropos of a sonnet of his own: 'Your ears are not so very fastidious; many people would not like words so prosaic and familiar in a sonnet as Islington and Hertfordshire.'[5] But Coleridge

---

[1] See the diary of Christopher Wordsworth, in the Appendix to *Social Life at the English Universities*.
[2] *Life and Correspondence* 1. 247.
[3] *Letters*, 1. 48.
[4] *Ibid.* 1. 4. 24-26, 28.
[5] *Ibid.* 1. 4.

had already expressed his liking for the real names of real things and people in more violent terms. 'For God's sake,' he writes to Southey in 1794,[1] 'let us have no more Bions or Gracchus's I abominate them! *Southey* is a name much more proper and handsome, and, I venture to prophecy, will be more *famous*.' Lamb's remarks on simplicity he seems to have received with humility. 'As to my own poetry,' he wrote to Thelwell, 'I do confess that it frequently, both in thought and language, deviates from "nature and simplicity,"' adding, characteristically, that Bowles is, with the exception of Burns, the only 'always natural poet' in our language.[2]

But meanwhile this new criticism was not modestly concealing itself from the public eye. Southey displayed the taste which had been 'meliorated' by Coleridge in some poetry that brought down on the head of him and his revolutionary friend the rather paternal admonitions of the *Critical Review*.[3] The *Critical Review* exactly represents the conventional attitude with regard to poetic diction. It is willing to grant that 'poetry has a language peculiar to itself' which excuses a very few deviations from the normal structure of prose; but this must not be carried too far. 'An occasional transposition creates variety and beauty. Mr. Southey gives frequent examples of this, by transposing the usual order of the verb and the nominative case. But we would advise him and Mr. Coleridge to introduce this practice with prudence, and but sparingly; otherwise they will rather obscure than illumine their verse and lose the charm of variety.' Having censured Southey for being too poetical in his syntax, the critic proceeds to remark that he is too prosaic in his tone. 'One leading rule for the style of poetry is that it should rise above the mere narrative of prose. Mr. Southey's lines are frequently prosaic, and

[1] *The Letters of Samuel Taylor Coleridge* I. 110.
[2] *Ibid.* I. 196.
[3] 17. 187—a review of Southey's *Joan of Arc*.

sometimes cannot even be read as verse.' This is exactly the attitude of the eighteenth century—no liberties with order, grammar, and syntax; but a vocabulary raised above prose, and verse that always scans in the one approved fashion. The critic also doubts whether Southey and Coleridge are justified in seeking variety of metre, citing for disapproval the lines;

> Now was the noon of night, and all was still,
> Save where the *sentinel paced on his watch*
> *Humming a broken tune.*

Such liberties, says the critic, 'grate on a correct ear.' He hopes Mr. Southey and Mr. Coleridge will be more careful in the future.

To such criticism as this Coleridge made a saucy reply. In the *Monthly Magazine,* whose aim was to print good articles that no other periodical would take, and to improve the quality of verse, he prints a rather charming little idyll, and entitles it: *Reflections on entering Active Life, A Poem which affects not to be Poetry.*[1] Though affecting not to be poetry, the poem is certainly worthy of quotation in full. But only the first few lines of it can be given here:

> Low was our pretty cot; the tallest rose
> Peep'd at our chamber-window. We could hear
> (At silent noon, and eve, and early morn)
> The sea's faint murmur; in the open air
> Our myrtles blossom'd, and across the porch
> Thick jasmines twin'd: the little landscape round
> Was green and woody, and refreshed the eye.

Here is the simplicity of style that Wordsworth was later to make famous!

About the same time there appeared in the *Monthly Magazine* a brief but very able article,[2] in which the sub-

---
[1] *The Monthly Magazine* 2. 732.
[2] 'Is Verse Essential to Poetry'? (2. 452).

stance of the Preface to the *Lyrical Ballads* and the Appendix on Poetic Diction is plainly anticipated. Whether Coleridge was responsible for it or not, it certainly reflects his opinions at this time. Verse, the writer decides, is not essential to poetry. The arguments with which he supports this thesis must be quoted at some length: 'Those writers appear to have approached nearest to a true definition of poetry, who have understood it to be the immediate offspring of a vigorous imagination and quick sensibility, and have called it the language of fancy and passion.[1] . . . In a rude state of nature, before the art of versification was known, men felt strong passions and expressed them strongly.[2] Their language would be bold and figurative; it would be vehement and abrupt; sometimes under the impulse of the gentle and the tender, or the gay and joyous passions, it would flow in a kind of wild and unfettered melody, for under such impressions, melody is natural to man. . . . The character of poetry, which may seem most to require that it be limited to verse is its appropriate diction. It will be admitted that metaphorical language, being more impressive than general terms, is best suited to poetry. That excited state of mind, which poetry supposes, naturally prompts a figurative style. But the language of fancy, sentiment, and passion is not peculiar to verse. Whatever is the natural and proper expression of any conception or feeling in metre is its natural and proper expression in prose.[3] All beyond this is a departure

---

[1] 'For all good poetry is the spontaneous overflow of powerful feeling.'—Preface to the *Lyrical Ballads*.

[2] 'The earliest poets of all nations generally wrote from passion excited by real events. . . . Feeling powerfully as they did, their language was daring and figurative.'—Appendix to the *Lyrical Ballads*, 1802.

[3] 'A large portion of every good poem can in no respect differ from that of prose. . . . It may be safely affirmed that there neither is nor can be any *essential* difference between the language of prose and metrical composition.'—*Ibid.* 1802.

from the true principles of taste. If the artificial diction of modern poetry would be improper on similar occasions in prose, it is equally improper in verse. In support of this opinion, the appeal may be made, not only to the general sense of impropriety, but to those most perfect models of fine writing, the Greek poets. The language of these great masters is always so consonant to nature, that, thrown out of rhythm, it would become the proper expression of the same sentiment in prose. If modern poetry will seldom bear to be brought to the same taste [test?], it is because the taste of the modern has been refined to a degree of fastidiousness which leads them to prefer the meretricious ornaments of art to the genuine simplicity of nature. . . . It obviously follows from the point established in this paper that the terms *poetry* and *prose* are incorrectly opposed to each other. *Verse* is properly the contrary of prose; and because poetry speaks the language of passion and sentiment, and philosophy speaks the language of reason, these two terms should be considered as contraries, and writing should be divided, not into poetry and prose, but into poetry and philosophy.'[1]

This is obviously the germ of the Preface to the *Lyrical Ballads*. But there is another interesting connection between the *Monthly Magazine* of 1796 and the *Lyrical Ballads*. In March of this year appeared William Taylor's translation of Bürger's *Lenore* into the language of Percy's *Reliques*. Lamb, always on the lookout for poetry that met his ideal of imaginative simplicity, eagerly called Coleridge's attention to it: 'Have you seen the ballad called "Leonore" in the second number of the *Monthly Magazine?*' he

[1] 'I here use the word Poetry (though against my own judgment) as opposed to the word Prose, and synonymous with metrical composition. But much confusion has been introduced into criticism by this contradistinction of Poetry and Prose, instead of the more philosophical one of Poetry and Matter of Fact, or Science. The only strict antithesis to Prose is Metre.'—Note to the Preface to the *Lyrical Ballads*.

writes.[1] 'If you have! ! ! ! ! ! ! ! There is another fine song, from the same author (Berger) in the 3rd No., of scarce inferior merit.' This translation made me a poet, said Scott. It is very likely that it made Wordsworth and Coleridge the poets of the *Lyrical Ballads*. If so, we have a very interesting connection between the quaint readings of Lamb, the theories of Coleridge, and the natural artistic instincts of Wordsworth. Certainly the name Bürger seems to have been coupled with that of Percy in the minds of Wordsworth and Coleridge from the beginning. The *Ancient Mariner*, the first of the *Lyrical Ballads*, and the one which suggested the writing of the others, is obviously influenced by the cadence and the style of Taylor's translation, and was to be published in the *Monthly Magazine* where *Leonora* had appeared. The decision of Wordsworth and Coleridge to study in Germany, the fact that one of the first things that Wordsworth did there was to buy a copy, not only of Percy's *Reliques*, but of Bürger's ballads,[2] added to the fact that one of the authors especially discussed by Wordsworth with Klopstock was Bürger[3]—all suggest that the German poet may have been responsible for the interest of the young poets in his English original. This evidence is strengthened by Wordsworth's remarks in the *Essay Supplementary to the Preface* concerning Percy's collection, 'This work did not steal silently into the world, as is evident from the number of legendary tales that appeared not long after its publication, and had been modeled, as the authors persuaded themselves, after the old Ballad. The compilation was, however, ill suited to the then existing state of city society; and Dr. Johnson, 'mid the little senate to which he gave laws, was not sparing in his exertions to make it an object of contempt. The

[1] *Works of Charles and Mary Lamb*, ed. Lucas (1802) 6. 38.
[2] Knight, *Life of Wordsworth* 1. 170.
[3] See Wordsworth's account of the conversation with Klopstock, quoted by Coleridge in *Satyrane's Letters.—Biographia Literaria*, ed. Shawcross, 2. 177.

critic triumphed, the legendary imitators were deservedly disregarded, and, as undeservedly, their ill-imitated models sank, in this country, into temporary neglect; while Bürger, and other able writers of Germany, were composing with the aid of inspiration thence derived, poems which were the delight of the German nation.' Then follows a comparison between the style of Bürger and that of Percy's collection.

But whether Lamb, acting through Coleridge, gave the first impulse to Wordsworth's interest in the popular ballads or not, the influence upon the new ideals of his delicate instinct and out-of-the-way readings must not be ignored. His interests at this time were much more exclusively literary than those of Coleridge, who could not help deviating into politics and philosophy. He was always ready to bring his adventurous friend down from the cloud-wrapped heights of Neoplatonism to a practical question of style, and to point out, not the courses of the stars, but delightful little bypaths among old and forgotten books. Thus, while he did not provide a theory of style, he continually furnished the materials and the standard for it. He would flit from poem to poem, choosing with almost unerring tact the 'genuine, sweet, and clear flowers of expression,' and avoiding by instinct the blooms of the hot-house. Being thus sensitive, he possessed a nature peculiarly 'capable of excitement without the application of gross and violent stimulants,' and loved what was simple and natural with the immediate response of a fine temperament. Hence he scarcely needed to look beyond himself for the principles of criticism. What shocked or displeased him or left him cold was probably bad or false; what delighted him was probably good and genuine. In all his remarks there is this delicate egotism—this consciousness that he carries the touchstone within himself. The ideal of simplicity in accordance with which he criticised Coleridge's early poems was a matter of taste, not the result of philosophical thought. Such an ideal could make no permanent appeal either to Coleridge or to Wordsworth; but it furnished a guide and a check to their bolder and more philosophical genius. The interest in the elder poets, especially, seems to have been Lamb's contribution to the cause. It was he who furnished Wordsworth with the library of old poems and plays which was, perhaps, the strongest and purest influence upon his work between 1800 and 1807.[1] To the simplicity of Coleridge and Southey, which was beginning to disturb the periodicals of the day, he added his own modest contributions, in the form of sonnets after the manner of Bowles. Some of these were appearing in the *Monthly Magazine* about the time Wordsworth went to Bristol[2] to meet those 'two remarkable youths, Southey and Coleridge.'

Thus it may be seen that, from the stimulating centre furnished by Coleridge's argumentative and contagious speech and manner, there were radiating lines of influence, in Southey, in Lamb, in the *Monthly Magazine*—not to mention minor disciples like Thelwell and Lloyd—which all tended to spread the ideal of a more simple and truly poetical expression. Poetry must no longer be distinguished from prose by external marks of language; its beauty must be something higher—not dress and jewelry adorning it from without, but a spirit illuminating and transfiguring it from within. This spirit had as yet no name. Coleridge and Lamb called it passion, or imagination, or fancy, but without being quite sure of the term that most clearly expressed it. However, they both thought they could distinguish it when they found it, and sought for it always in their enterprising reading. But when Coleridge met Wordsworth, he at once recognized in him the quality which he considered the nameless essential of poetry; and then and there began the second stage in this noble discussion.

[1] *Letters of Charles Lamb* I. 160.
[2] *The Letters of Samuel Taylor Coleridge.*

CHAPTER 5.

COLERIDGE AND WORDSWORTH.

What Wordsworth brought to the discussion already so well begun we can only guess from the character that it immediately assumed. He seems to have interpreted the more abstract reasoning of Coleridge in the light of his old imaginative love of nature, and his more recent interest in the psychology and the sorrows of the poor and lowly.

Of this 'still, sad music of humanity' there are many echoes in the verse written after he left Cambridge. Indeed there is already a hint of it in the *Evening Walk* and the *Descriptive Sketches*—a hint more fully developed in the two poems, *The Female Vagrant* and *Salisbury Plain,* which were later combined in *Guilt and Sorrow.* The *Old Man Travelling*[1] and the narrative of the *Ruined Cottage*[2] have a similar motive. In the *Borderers,* composed as Wordsworth tells us in 1795-1796, he had also explored the more strange and curious processes in the mind which lead to the sorrows that so troubled him; and had, for the first time, endeavored to make his syntax reflect the movements of impassioned thought. The best thing in the *Borderers* is the language; it is a fine, clear, flexible imitation of actual speech, and, as such, anticipates the more special effort of the *Lyrical Ballads.* In this 'selection of the real language of men,' and, incidentally, of the language of Shakespeare, he seems to have attained, for the first time,[3] a perfect command of the English idiom. The

---

[1] Printed as *Animal Tranquillity and Decay* in the Oxford edition, which follows the last edition printed in Wordsworth's lifetime.

[2] Incorporated in the first book of the *Excursion*.

[3] The translation of Juvenal (reprinted in *Letters of the Wordsworth Family* I. 94-98) is more idiomatic than anything Wordsworth had written hitherto. No doubt this imitation of the 'real language of men,' as employed by the satirists, also helped him to attain a command of English phrase and syntax.

language of the poetic drama had always tended to bridge the gap between the formal written language and colloquial speech. In Wordsworth's development it seems to have prepared the way for the experiment of 1798.

Hence, when the frequent intercourse between the two poets began in 1797, Wordsworth was prepared to vitalize and illustrate the theories of Coleridge by his more intense and imaginative interest in the concrete facts of nature and human life. The two young men were alike in their natural bent toward philosophical criticism. Possessing at first a less unerring instinct for style than Lamb, they also possessed active and powerful intellects, which continually brought their personal tastes to the bar of judgment, and sought to find a basis for their own preferences in the fundamental characteristics of human nature. Accordingly, Coleridge's tendency to philosophical speculation, sportively or seriously rebuked by Lamb when it took a religious turn, and blithely disregarded under other circumstances, coincided with something in Wordsworth's own mind, and became the most vital element in their mutual discussion of the ideal of poetic expression towards which they had both been blindly groping. The scope of this new discussion is suggested in two incidental remarks by Coleridge and Wordsworth. Upon hearing Wordsworth recite his poem, *Salisbury Plain*, Coleridge was immediately impressed with Wordsworth's peculiar gift of making 'the familiar be as though it were not familiar,' of suggesting 'the depth and height of the ideal world' through the most common incidents of daily life. This seemed to him the diviner spirit of poetry which he had been seeking—the inward transfiguring grace.

'This excellence, which in all Mr. Wordsworth's writings is more or less predominant, and which constitutes the character of his mind, I no sooner felt, than I sought to understand. Repeated meditations led me first to suspect (and a more intimate analysis of the human faculties, their appropriate marks, functions, and effects, matured my conjecture into full conviction) that fancy and imagination were two distinct and widely differing faculties,' writes Coleridge.[1] This presupposes a whole theory of psychology as a basis for a theory of poetry—a theory which Wordsworth developed and utilized in his classification of his poems in accordance with the human faculties, and their 'appropriate marks, functions, and effects' therein illustrated. But Wordsworth's own indications of the scope of the talk that inspired the *Lyrical Ballads* go even further. He presupposes a historical survey of social psychology, as well as a thorough investigation of the development of language and literature. 'For to treat of the subject with the clearness and coherence of which I believe it susceptible,' he says, 'it would be necessary to give a full account of the present state of public taste in this country, and to determine how far this taste is healthy or depraved; which again could not be determined without pointing out in what manner language and the human mind act and react on each other, and without retracing the revolutions not of literature alone but likewise of society itself.'[2] This ambitious outline must always be borne in mind in criticizing any single statement concerning the language of poetry made by Coleridge or Wordsworth. Their utterances were not casual or arbitrary. They were part of a great, and, in general, a self-consistent whole, which was never completed in detail, but which always formed the background for any individual remark. The separate fragments of Wordsworth's literary criticism bear much the same relation to each other, and to an unwritten whole, as the shorter poems, the *Prelude,* and the *Excursion* bear to the projected *Recluse.*

This unwritten inquiry certainly included:

[1] *B. L.* 1. 60.
[2] Preface to the *Lyrical Ballads.*

1. An analysis of the poetic faculty in all its manifestations, with some inquiry not only into the nature of the feeling induced by poetry, but into the character of all natural phenomena which accidentally, as it were, produce a spiritual reaction analogous to that which the poet aims to produce or to reproduce.

2. The observation of the manner in which the poetic faculty expresses itself in unpremeditated speech—in those spontaneous associations of images, and deviations from the normal order and structure of language, for the sake of a special emphasis, which are called figures of speech.

3. The determination of the kind of words and phrases that have been the most universal and permanent expression of this faculty in English.

These three elements in the discussion are all suggested in the definition of the purpose of the *Lyrical Ballads* which Wordsworth gave in 1802—'to choose incidents and situations from common life, and to relate or describe them, throughout, as far as was possible in a selection of language really used by men, and, at the same time, to throw over them a certain colouring of imagination, whereby ordinary things should be presented to the mind in an unusual aspect; and, further, and above all, to make these incidents and situations interesting by tracing in them truely though not ostentatiously, the primary laws of our nature: chiefly as far as regards the manner in which we *associate ideas in a state of excitement.*' This is far from being a narrow definition of poetic style. Whether we say with Dryden, or Dryden's master, Longinus, or with John Dennis, that the language of poetry is the language of passion; or whether, with Aristotle, or Shelley, or Walter Pater, we emphasize the 'strangeness added to beauty' in the poet's style; or whether, with Horace, and the whole school of Latin-French criticism represented by Pope, we especially insist on the selective power of the poet, we can still find our definition included in that of

Wordsworth. But, while these three elements were all suggested in his criticism from the first, and implied in it to the last, there was a distinct shift of emphasis. The poetic development that began in 1798 with a defense of the language of the lower and middle classes of society ends with the preface on the language of imagination and fancy in 1815; and it is the last which is allowed to stand as an introduction to the poet's complete works for the rest of his life. The language of the *Lyrical Ballads* will not be entirely understood until we follow it to its maturity in *Laodamia* and the *Primrose of the Rock*.

This, unfortunately, we cannot do within the narrow limits of these pages. Nor can we trace the indebtedness of Wordsworth to the formal psychology and philosophy to which Coleridge introduced him—the theory of the association of ideas and the physiological origin of them in Hartley's *Observations on Man* and Darwin's *Zoönomia*, and the discussions of Spinoza which so troubled the inquisitive spy. The effect of this new reading on Wordsworth's diction alone was so extensive and remarkable that it demands an entirely separate treatment in connection with the *Prelude*, where the style so brilliantly exemplified in the *Lines written a Few Miles above Tintern Abbey* is carried to its height.[1] It is one of the miracles of poetry that lines which have taken such a hold on the popular imagination as these should be merely the result of setting to music the semi-technical vocabulary of treatises on physiology and psychology. But while it must not be forgotten that Tintern Abbey, no less than the true *Lyrical Ballads*, is an offshoot of the new effort and criticism, and that the style there displayed was developing side by side with the style of *The Thorn*, nevertheless we must confine ourselves, for the present, to the theories illustrated in the latter.

[1] See Beatty, *'Wordsworth and Hartley'*—*The Nation* 97. 51 ff.

However, since all three elements which we have distinguished in the theory of Wordsworth and Coleridge at this time affected the imitation of the language of the middle and lower classes, it is necessary to consider the various hints of the part that each of them played in the conversations of that time. They are all an effort to reinterpret and vitalize the familiar ideas of the eighteenth century. The old search for a universal language of poetry was begun anew, with a deeper faith that poetry is passion—that in the actual psychology of emotion is to be found the source and the standard of every legitimate poetical device.

1. *The Poetic Faculty—Imagination and Fancy.*

The discussion of imagination began, says Coleridge, with his attempt to analyze the peculiar quality in Wordsworth's poetic association of ideas, as compared with that of verse which might seem more clever and striking. The distinction which he and Wordsworth were elaborating and illustrating for the next twenty years is expressed by Wordsworth in his note to *The Thorn* in 1800: 'Superstitious men are almost always men of slow faculties and deep feelings; their minds are not loose, but adhesive; they have a reasonable share of imagination, by which I mean the faculty which produces impressive effects out of simple elements; but they are utterly destitute of fancy, the power by which pleasure and surprise are excited by sudden varieties of situation and by accumulated imagery.'

As Wordsworth illustrates the distinction by observing the minds of his humble neighbors, so Coleridge illustrates it by observing the mind of Wordsworth[1]: 'A poet's heart and intellect should be *combined,* intimately combined and unified with the great appearance of nature, and not merely held in solution and loose mixture with them, in the shape of formal similes. . . . It must occur to every reader

[1] *Letters of Samuel Taylor Coleridge* 1. 404-406.

that the Greeks in their religious poems address always the Numina Loci, the Genii, the Dryads, the Naiads, etc., etc. All natural objects were *dead*, mere hollow statues, but there was a Godkin or Goddessling *included* in each. In the Hebrew poetry you find nothing of this poor stuff, as poor in genuine imagination as it is mean in intellect. At best it is but fancy, or the aggregating faculty of the mind, not imagination, or the *modifying* and coadunating faculty. This the Hebrew poets appear to me to have possessed beyond all others, and next to them the English. In the Hebrew poets each thing has a life of its own, and yet they are all our life.'

These distinctions are undoubtedly Coleridge's; but the illustration of the effect of imagination could only have originated with Wordsworth. 'During the first year that Mr. Wordsworth and I were neighbours,' writes Coleridge,[1] 'our conversations turned frequently on the two cardinal points of poetry, the power of exciting the sympathy of the reader by faithful adherence to the truth of nature, and the power of giving the interest of novelty by the modifying colors of the imagination. *The sudden charm, which accidents of light and shade, which moon-light or sun-set, diffused over a known and familiar landscape, appeared to represent the practicability of combining both.*' This at once recalls the recognition of the transfiguring power of the light of sunset which had been Wordsworth's first poetic inspiration at fourteen, as well as the theme of much of his descriptive writing, and the subject of his only piece of literary criticism hitherto. No doubt, as he spoke to Coleridge of these things, he remembered the curious experiences of his boyhood—how the lonely figure of the shepherd on the hilltop, ennobled by mist and light, had flashed upon his eye, a strange and godlike form; how the unexpected sight of the black crag had stirred and troubled

[1] *B. L.* 2. 5. The italics are mine.

him for days with thoughts of huge and mighty forms that do not move like living men. He knew that the shepherd was but a poor, inglorious creature, and that the black crag was only a 'rocky protuberance,' as Dr. Johnson would say; but such experiences were like the waking of old memories, or the sudden vision of strange spiritual worlds beyond the veil of sense. These shadowy exaltations were moments of fear and joy and astonished self-revelation. If his poetry could produce on other minds the effect that the 'poetry of nature' produced on his—then the great problem of the source and end of imaginative art was solved. This new interpretation of the boyhood experience that first made him a poet is the theme of the *Prelude,* which was begun shortly after this time, and is throughout an illustration of the new conception of imagination. Much that he there writes down for Coleridge he must already have said in the autobiographical outpourings natural in the beginning of an enthusiastic friendship.

The different phases of the new theory of imagination are illustrated in *The Thorn.* 'This,' Wordsworth said,[1] 'grew out of my observing on the ridge of Quantock Hill, on a stormy day, a thorn which I had often passed, in calm and bright weather, without noticing it. I said to myself, "Cannot I by some invention do as much to make this Thorn permanently an impressive object as the storm has made it to my eyes this moment?"' In attempting to do this he chose, as a medium of communication to the reader, the simple mind that he describes as imaginative rather than fanciful—a mind in which a single overwhelming emotion, uniting with all the dim sense of wonder characteristic of children and unlearned men, gives unity and intensity to its impressions, as the storm seems to unify and transfigure the outstanding features of a landscape. This single emotion expresses itself in a tendency to recur to the one absorb-

---

[1] See *Memoirs* I. 110.

ing idea, and to bring everything else into relation with it; hence the elaborate repetitions in the poem.

To heighten the coloring of imagination, Wordsworth does not hesitate to make use of distinctly romantic suggestions—such as the stirring of the moss on the child's grave beneath the spade, and the haunting vision of the baby's face. Such associated ideas, borrowed from literature very different from that which he essayed to write, are also used in *The Idiot Boy* and *Peter Bell,* where all the artistic effects of moonlight, well known to cheap romancers, and images of horseman ghosts and blooming wood-boys and 'spires and mosques and abbey windows' are made to attend on the lowly figures of the poor idiot boy and the disreputable potter.

2. *Figures of Speech.*

On the subject of imagination, Wordsworth and Coleridge seemed to be in agreement from the first. With language it was not so. As early as 1802 Coleridge began to suspect that 'somewhere or other there is a radical difference in our theoretical opinions concerning poetry.'[1] This radical difference seems to consist in their respective use of the term *language.* To Coleridge language meant words considered in themselves, and especially in their syntactical relations[2]; to Wordsworth it meant the whole imaginative expression of the thought—which, in most cases, meant figures of speech. This he probably did not at first realize. Before 1802 his use of the terms *language, phraseology, diction,* etc., seems to be rather loose. No doubt he was continually influenced by Coleridge's more distinct interpretation of these words.

But when, in the Appendix on Poetic Diction, he really undertakes to define his terms, several difficulties in the

[1] *Letters of Samuel Taylor Coleridge* 2. 386-387.
[2] *B. L.* 2. 39-49.

Preface of 1800 are at once cleared. Obviously he is not talking about vocabulary and syntax. Primarily he is talking about figures of speech and rhetorical devices. When, in 1802, he condemns the lines,

> These valleys and rocks never heard,
> Ne'er sighed at the sound of a knell,
> Or smiled when the Sabbath appeared,

as 'vicious poetic diction,' we see that he cannot mean the choice or arrangement of words. *Valleys, rocks, sighed, sound, smiled, Sabbath, appeared*—what words could be more homely or more specific; what grammatical construction or what order of words could be more straightforward or simple? What he is actually condemning is the pathetic fallacy, the false and frigid personification of valleys and rocks as creatures that could sigh or smile. This he makes plain enough. The two lines, 'Ne'er sighed at the sound,' etc., he says, are an instance of the 'language of passion wrested from its proper use, . . . and applied upon an occasion which does not justify such violent expression.' It is therefore 'vicious poetic diction.'

The meaning that Wordsworth here makes so explicit seems to be more or less implicit in what he says concerning language. 'Yet morning smiles the busy race to cheer' is at least as simple in vocabulary, and almost as direct in construction, as the line, 'A different object do these eyes require.' In both cases there is a slight departure from the normal order of prose. Yet Wordsworth condemns the first, and approves the second. What he apparently objects to is not the words as such, but the frigid periphrasis of 'busy race,' and the stale personification in 'morning smiles.' In other words, his criticism, from first to last, concerns not poetic diction, primarily, but poetic imagery. He is interested in words in so far as words are also metaphors.

When we make this mental transference, substituting imagery for language, we begin to understand the statement that the peasant daily communes with the best objects from which the best part of language is usually derived, and that 'the language arising out of repeated experience and regular feelings is a more permanent and a far more philosophical language than that frequently substituted for it by poets.' As Hartley had taught him, the language of men is vitally metaphorical. We continually express one idea in terms of another, and explain images by other associated images. In the figurative expressions and illustrations that men daily use—especially when strong feeling puts a strain on the ordinary resources of language—are found the germs of poetic art.

'Similes, fables, parables, allegories, etc.,' writes Hartley,[1] 'are all instances of natural analogies improved and set off by art. And they have this common to them all, that the properties, beauties, perfections, desires, or defects and aversions, which adhere by association to the simile, parable, or emblem of any kind, are insensibly, as it were, transferred upon the thing represented. Hence the passions are moved to good or evil, speculation is turned into practice, and either some important truth felt and realized, or some error and vice gilded over and recommended.' We cannot speak of a 'rosy face,' or a 'friendly greeting,' or a 'cool manner' without speaking metaphorically; and the most permanent and expressive metaphors are those which are founded upon the most universal phenomena—upon those which are connected with 'our moral sentiments and animal sensations, with the operations of the elements, and the appearance of the visible universe; with storm and sunshine, with the revolutions of the seasons, with cold and heat, with loss of friends and kindred, with injuries and resentments, gratitude and hope, fear and sorrow.'[2]

When Wordsworth's term, *language,* is interpreted to mean *metaphor,* primarily—the expression of one experi-

[1] *On Man* I. 297.
[2] Preface to the *Lyrical Ballads* 1802.

ence in terms of another—we begin to understand wherein the language of the present has the advantage over that of the cheap poet. The poet talks about the 'flames' of love and the 'lightnings' of the fair lady's eyes; but both the popular poet and his readers, according to Wordsworth in his early republicanism, are too busy with 'routs, dinners, morning calls, hurry from door to door, from street to street, on foot or in carriage,'[1] to give more than a passing glance to any actual flame or lightning. They take these phenomena on faith; the images are handed down from poet to poet, growing a little more general and more faded with each transmission. But the peasant, even the peasant of little imagination, living in the presence of storms and lightnings, sitting without emotion, hope, or aim, in the loved presence of his cottage fire, receives into his heart a clear image of these things through long observation and association; and hence, if he compares a feeling to a flame, he associates a distinct image with the idea of flame, and the metaphor is true and vital. It was this clearness and reality of imagery that Wordsworth was trying to bring back into poetry. 'I do not know how to give my reader a more exact notion of the style in which it was my wish and intention to write,' he says,[2] 'than by informing him that I have at all times endeavored to look steadily at my subject.'

Of course the poet's choice of words is vitally affected by the choice of metaphors, and by the rigorous exclusion of figures of speech which do not really represent the object described, or the nature of the feeling which, in moments of excitement, colors and even distorts the perception of the object. And when the poet is speaking in the character of an excited peasant, dramatic fitness also limits the vocabulary. The observation of the speech of simple men certainly affects the words, and especially the syntax, of the *Lyrical Ballads,* as we shall see. Nevertheless, so little has Words-

[1] Letter to Lady Beaumont, May 21, 1807 (*L. W. F.* 1. 302).
[2] Preface to the *Lyrical Ballads.*

worth's famous theory to do with words in themselves that it may be questioned whether it fairly excludes the use of such a word as *incommunicable* in Margaret's lament,[1] so often cited as an example of the inconsistency of his theory with his practice:

> Perhaps some dungeon hears thee groan,
> Maimed, mangled by inhuman men;
> Or thou upon the desert thrown
> Inheritest the lion's den;
> Or hast been summoned to the deep,
> Thou, thou and all thy mates to keep
> An incommunicable sleep.

This is not Margaret's language, the critics point out with glee, 'incommunicable' not being in that simple woman's vocabulary. But if the association of ideas is true and vital—if the words are a real expression of the mother's wistful thought: 'They are asleep; but they cannot give their sleep to me or to any one'—then the *curiosa felicitas* of the adjective in this connection, its mournful sonority, its vague Shakespearean suggestions, have nothing to do with the matter. There is nothing implying wide experience or intellectual culture in Margaret's thought; it is one of those strange intuitive associations of ideas that come to children and poets and the simplest hearts. It is truly her method of expression, although the poet's vocabulary supplies the word.

While this extension of the word *language* undoubtedly explains much of Wordsworth's criticism and practice, it cannot be asserted that he always used the term in this sense. In the *Lyrical Ballads* of 1798, in particular, he was deliberately imitating the speech of the lower classes, with all its peculiarities of vocabulary and syntax, as we shall see. He never could define his terms to the satisfaction of his friends. Coleridge did not know what he meant by

[1] *The Affliction of Margaret* 50-56 (Oxford edition, p. 117).

language; nor Crabb Robinson what he understood by *imagination.* Perhaps it was this conscious difficulty in translating his own rather emotional and poetical thinking into the terms of the intellect that prevented him from writing more criticism. But in his use of the term *language* he was undoubtedly influenced also by a very interesting theory of Coleridge's.

3. *The Universal Language of Poetry.*

This notion, which is mentioned in the Advertisement of 1798[1] as the opinion of the author of the *Ancient Mariner,* and is suggested in a footnote added in Coleridge's handwriting to the Preface of 1800, was probably the result of the reading of the ballads. Observing, with the possible help of Wordsworth, that the most ancient of these poems more nearly resembled the actual colloquial speech of 1797 than did the average verse of that year, Coleridge was led to the opinion that there is a permanent body of English words and idioms, denoting universal phenomena and experiences, which have remained comparatively unchanged since the time of Chaucer.[2] This is the universal language of poetry, for it represents the permanent and changeless elements in human life. If we free the rustic speech from a few merely local elements, and the popular ballads from a very few archaisms, there remains much the same residuum; and the residuum proves, on examination, to be a

---

[1] 'The Rime of the Ancyent Marinere was professedly written in imitation of the style, as well as the spirit of the elder poets, but with a few exceptions, the Author believes that the language adopted there has been equally intelligible for three centuries.'—Advertisement to the Lyrical Ballads.

[2] 'It is worth while to observe that the affecting parts of Chaucer are almost always expressed in language pure and universally intelligible to this day.'—A Description of the Wordsworth and Coleridge MSS. in the Possession of Mr. T. Norton Longman, p. 19.

See also Hazlitt, *My First Acquaintance with the Poets (Literary Remains* 2. 392).

body of words common to Chaucer and to almost any Englishman of the year 1797. He who can use this concrete, emotional, and idiomatic speech with all the power of which it is capable has found the true and lasting basis of poetic diction.

This theory both Wordsworth and Coleridge tried to illustrate, but with one characteristic difference; for in the *Ancient Mariner* Coleridge contrives to retain a few romantic archaisms, and Wordsworth, in the *Lyrical Ballads,* keeps some special realistic features of the speech of the lower and middle classes of society. With *The Ancient Mariner* we are not here concerned. But Wordsworth's effort must be carefully analyzed.

CHAPTER 6.

THE LYRICAL BALLADS.

Although Wordsworth's theory of poetic diction had a sounder basis in literary tradition and in psychology than an ignorant world of letters was prepared to admit, his own application of it, in its first extreme form, was very limited in time and in extent. Only in the Advertisement to the *Lyrical Ballads* of 1798 does he say that he means to employ the 'language of conversation in the middle and lower classes of society'; and only in this volume does he actually succeed in doing so. But even here he makes use of this language simply as an 'experiment,' and clearly indicates that the experiment applies only to a part—though a major part—of the collection.

The poems composing the minority, not included under Wordsworth's definition of his purpose, are easily determined. Apart from the contributions of Coleridge, and apart from Tintern Abbey, which, as Wordsworth himself indicates, was composed in the loftier and more impassioned strain of the ode,[1] they prove to be the poems written before 1797—the *Lines left upon a Seat in a Yew-Tree, The Female Vagrant,* the *Lines written near Richmond,* and the *Convict*—none of which show any trace of the ballad-literature. One other poem in the volume shows virtually nothing of this influence. This is the *Old Man Travelling,* which occupies a unique place in the first edition. It is the only representative of a type of delineation of rustic life in blank verse which developed side by side with the *Lyrical Ballads,* but which does not otherwise appear in print till the volumes of 1800. The remaining poems in the first edition form a homogeneous group, clearly reflecting the

---

[1] See note on Tintern Abbey in the *Lyrical Ballads,* 1802-1805, reprinted by Hutchinson in the Oxford edition, p. 901.

literary influence suggested in the title, and the theory of poetic diction suggested in the Advertisement. *They* are the real experiment—the attempt to co-ordinate the artless art of the ballads with Wordsworth's own observation of the psychological processes underlying the speech of simple men; the rest are merely poems written in various moods and in various styles.

This group of the true *Lyrical Ballads* falls into four main divisions:

1. Philosophical and narrative poems in the metre, and, to a certain extent, the style of the ballads, but wholly differing from them in substance.

    (a) Philosophical and reflective poems, in which the narrative element is at a minimum:

Lines written in Early Spring
Lines written at a Small Distance from my House
Expostulation and Reply
The Tables Turned.

    (b) Narrative poems in the nature of simple anecdotes designed to illustrate a philosophical truth that is far less simple:

We are Seven
Anecdote for Fathers
Simon Lee.

2. Narrative and lyrical poems, less recondite in thought, but written in a 'more impressive metre than is usual in the Ballads'[1]:

    (a) Poems more narrative than lyrical:
Goody Blake and Harry Gill
The Idiot Boy
(*Peter Bell*).

    (b) Poems in which the lyrical element tends to pre-

---

[1] Preface, 1800, p. xxxv.

dominate, or does wholly predominate (characterized by the use of the refrain):

The Thorn
The Last of the Flock
The Mad Mother
The Complaint of the Forsaken Indian Woman.

The last group most obviously illustrate Wordsworth's suggested definition of a lyrical ballad, as a narrative poem in which the 'feeling therein developed gives importance to the action and situation, and not the action and situation to the feeling,'[1] though this description applies to all the poems.

In these several groups of poems, there are some distinct peculiarities of language which are directly traceable to the combined influence of the *Reliques* and the speech of rustics, and which, for better or for worse, had a far-reaching influence upon Wordsworth's poetic diction.

As we have already said, by language Wordsworth apparently meant, not vocabulary alone, but the whole body and dress of thought—all that appears to the eye and ear when (if we may say this without irreverence) the word becomes flesh, and takes its place among things that have a material, as well as a spiritual existence. But the unit of expression, for all practical purposes, is generally the individual term—words, in the usual sense; and hence any influence affecting language does first of all affect the vocabulary. Accordingly, we will begin with the vocabulary of these *Lyrical Ballads,* and proceed thence to the more important matters of syntax, and of narrative and lyrical technique.

1. Vocabulary.

At first glance, the vocabulary of the *Lyrical Ballads* does not seem to be notable. Apart from a number of colloquial expressions, it is a pure, clear vocabulary of con-

[1] Preface, 1800, p. xvii.

crete words, neither more nor less simple than the language of the majority of poems in the *Oxford Book of English Verse*. But when we examine it in the light of the discussions of Wordsworth and Coleridge, even this fact becomes interesting.

As has already been said, the two poets had some notion that there was a permanent body of English words—the names of common things and universal emotions—which had remained comparatively unaltered since the days of Chaucer. This was the generally intelligible language of poetry which the eighteenth century had always endeavored to discover—a language 'simple, sensuous, and passionate.' This contention is fully justified by the *Lyrical Ballads*. Although Wordsworth's avowed effort is to imitate the language that he daily hears on the lips of unlearned men, stanza after stanza of the most typical Wordsworthian verse in this volume contain only words that may be found in Skeat's glossary to Chaucer. This is true, for instance, of the description of the little cottage girl:

> I met a little cottage girl,
>   She was eight years old, she said;
> Her hair was thick with many a curl[1]
>   That clustered round her head,[2]

and of 'the wonderful lines—*quam nihil ad genium naucleri*' which Hutchinson chooses as the supreme example of a case in which the 'lineaments of the poet peep out through his clumsy disguise'[3]:

> At all times of the day or night
> This wretched woman thither goes,
> *And she is known to every star,*
> *And every wind that blows.*[4]

---

[1] Occurs in Chaucer's poetry as *crul, crulle,* meaning *curly.*
[2] *We are Seven* 5-8.
[3] *Lyrical Ballads,* ed. Hutchinson, p. 240.
[4] *The Thorn* 67-70.

THE LYRICAL BALLADS 145

Even when the poet is writing more philosophically, he still seems to find the vocabulary of Chaucer not inadequate. In the stanza,

> Sweet is the lore which Nature brings;
> Our meddling intellect
> Misshapes the beauteous forms of things;
> —We murder to dissect,[1]

only the word 'dissect'[2] is entirely unknown to his master. Of course there are many cases in which this is not so. *Rustic*[3] in the line, 'She had a *rustic* woodland air,' and *intermitted*[4] in the line, 'And held such *intermitted* talk,' are not Chaucerian. The remarkable thing is that he should have come so near the vocabulary of the 'first finder of our fair language,' when he was writing in accordance with a theory in which the imitation of Chaucer was merely an incidental suggestion by Coleridge. It is certainly a proof of the essential soundness of this new conception of the universal language of poetry that, after so many centuries, some of the most characteristic expressions of an imagination so individual as that of Wordsworth should be strictly in the vocabulary of Chaucer.[5]

While this attempt to find the really permanent element in the English language was undoubtedly the most valuable

---

[1] *The Tables Turned* 25-28.

[2] The earliest occurrence of this word noted in the *N. E. D.* is in Topsell, *Serpents* 621 (1607).

[3] The earliest occurrence of this word noted in the *N. E. D.* is in Palladadius *On Husbandry* I. 1027 (*c.* 1440).

[4] The earliest occurrence of the word in this sense noted in the *N. E. D.* is in Wyatt, *Death of the Countess Pembroke* 421-422 (1542).

[5] Of the words in the *Concordance* to the poems of Wordsworth, I estimate that about 60 per cent occur, in some form, in the poetry of Chaucer; about 68 per cent. in the poetry of Milton; about 80 per cent in the poetry of Spenser; and 90 per cent in the poetry of Shakespeare.

feature of the new theory, there is abundant evidence that Wordsworth himself was more especially interested in the artistic possibilities of exclusively colloquial turns of expression. These occur chiefly in the poems in which there is a somewhat dramatic attempt to imitate the manners, as well as the emotions, of humble characters. By far the largest proportion of them is found in *Goody Blake and Harry Gill* and *The Idiot Boy*, as well as in the later, unpublished poem of *The Tinker*, which belongs to the same type, and in the first edition of *Peter Bell*, which, though not printed until 1819, is a true lyrical ballad. Where the emotional and lyrical element begins to predominate, these colloquialisms tend to disappear, as in *The Thorn* and *The Last of the Flock*. This is a rather interesting fact—a possibly unintentional illustration of Wordsworth's own belief that the universal language is the language of the heart. One would naturally expect to find colloquialisms in a dramatic lyric, where the poet is speaking through the mouth of a humble character, rather than in a narrative, where he speaks in his own person. But the half-humorous observation of external manners lowers the style, while emotion raises and universalizes it. This is especially true in the case of *The Mad Mother*, whose pathetic song is not sullied by any of the curious importations from vulgar speech that are so frequent in *The Idiot Boy*.

The colloquialisms are of two sorts. There are words which are chiefly confined to speech; and there are words which, though frequent in literature and capable of beautiful and noble uses, are employed in the *Lyrical Ballads* in a manner not common outside of conversation. The colloquialisms of the first type have generally an onomatopoetic value. In the earlier descriptive poems, Wordsworth had already showed a special interest in words expressive of sound. To those which he there employed he has now added a choice collection of more homely creations of this kind:

THE LYRICAL BALLADS 147

> Said Peter to the groaning Ass,
> But I will *bang* your bones.[1]

> With his visage grim and sooty,
> *Bumming, bumming, bumming.*[2]

> *Burr, burr,* now Johnny's lips they *burr.*[3]

> The owlets hoot, the owlets *curr.*[4]

In such cases, as will be noticed, he often increases the effect of the word by repetition:

> She lifts the knocker—*rap, rap, rap.*[5]

> Then his hammer he rouzes,
> *Batter! batter! batter!*[6]

> His teeth they *chatter, chatter* still.[7]

In addition to the words thus definitely expressing sound, there is a large number of words more vaguely onomatopoetic in character, all of which have the same homely rhythm, dimly suggestive of *Mother Goose*—*fiddle-faddle, hob-nob, hurly-burly, flurry, bowzes, pother,* etc. In such lines as

> Fond lovers, yet not quite hob nob[8];

> It dried her body like a cinder,
> And almost turned her brain to tinder,[9]

---

[1] *Peter Bell* 199-200. Reprinted from the edition of 1819 in *Lyrical Ballads,* ed. Hutchinson, pp. 137 ff.
[2] *The Tinker* 37.
[3] *The Idiot Boy* 107.
[4] *Ibid.* 114.
[5] *Ibid.* 258.
[6] *The Tinker* 12.
[7] *Goody Blake and Harry Gill* 12.
[8] *The Idiot Boy* 299-300.
[9] *The Thorn* 131-132. Altered in 1815 to:

> A fire was kindled in her breast,
> Which might not burn itself to rest.

there is a touch of honest vulgarity which is characteristic of *The Tinker* throughout. Nothing in his published work so completely reveals the strain of rustic good nature in Wordsworth, unmodified by any higher touches of poetry, as this piece, with its cheerful rude metre and unpolished phrases[1]:

> Who leads a happy life
> If it's not the merry Tinker?
> Not too old to have a wife;
> Not too much a thinker.
> . . . .
> Right before the Farmer's door
> Down he sits; his brows he knits;
> Then his hammer he rouzes;
>   Batter! batter! batter!
> He begins to clatter;
> And while the work is going on
>   Right good ale he bowzes.[2]

But this poem was withheld from print, and the style employed in it was seldom allowed to appear in Wordsworth's poetry after the *Lyrical Ballads*. In *Benjamin the Waggoner*, his most successful attempt at humor, something of a broadly, rudely playful sympathy with the foibles of a humble sinner is retained; but it is expressed in language so pure and limpid that it would not disgrace Chaucer's own well of English undefiled. Many of the colloquial words just listed were omitted in correction,[3] and do not appear in the *Concordance* at all. Others were never used after the appearance of the *Lyrical Ballads*.[4] Words-

---

[1] Reprinted in *A Description of the Wordsworth and Coleridge Manuscripts in the Possession of Mr. T. Norton Longman*, pp. 67-68; cf. Knight, *Life of Wordsworth* I. 310.

[2] *The Tinker* 1-15.

[3] *Bang, fiddle-faddle, tinder,* etc., were omitted in revision, and never employed again.

[4] *Burr, curr, hob-nob, hurly-burly, flurry* (in the phrase *in a flurry*), etc., are employed only in the *Lyrical Ballads*. *Bowzes, batter, bumming,* etc., occur only in the unpublished poem, *The Tinker*.

worth eliminated the over-colloquial elements from his vocabulary, as carefully as he removed the pedantic or bookish expressions from the early descriptive poems. The former are as little characteristic of his mature style as the latter.

Most of the colloquial words had some artistic justification in their onomatopoetic value; but this can hardly be said of many phrases of the same type—'not *a whit* the better he,' 'I fear you're in a *dreadful way*,' 'in a *mighty fret*,' 'in a *mighty flurry*,'

> *Sad case,* as you may think,
> For very cold to go to bed,
> And then for cold not *sleep a wink,*

etc. Most of these also were rejected by Wordsworth's mature taste.[1] Nothing could give a better idea of the almost uniform nobility of his style than to look up words like *dreadful, fret, mighty,* etc., in the Concordance, and to find the quotation from the *Lyrical Ballads* standing out in lonely contrast to such lines as

> Implores the *dreadful* untried sleep of death.[2]
>
> Dim *dreadful* faces through the gloom appear.[3]
>
> I love the brooks which down their channels *fret.*[4]
>
> And see the children sport upon the shore
> And hear the *mighty* waters rolling evermore.[5]
>
> And these perennial bowers and murmuring pines
> Be gracious as the music and the bloom
> And all the *mighty* ravishment of spring.[6]

[1] None of the expressions here mentioned occurs in Wordsworth's poetry outside of the *Lyrical Ballads.*
[2] *D. S.* Quarto 643.
[3] *Ibid.* 650.
[4] *Immortality* 196.
[5] *Ibid.* 170-171.
[6] *Lady! the songs of Spring were in the grove* 12-14.

This fullness of content, this imaginative dignity, are the really typical features of Wordsworth's style, whether he is borrowing his actual words from a peasant or from Shakespeare. This he himself realized more and more.[1] However, at the beginning, his interest in the poor and lowly made him forget that he was using them as types, and their language as a universal expression of universal feelings, rather than as an external mark of a single class, and a single stage of culture. When he takes a line of genuine poetry—of pure and emotional English—directly from the lips of a peasant,[2] as he sometimes does, we are grateful indeed for the gift; but where this essentially poetical character is lacking, the language of the country villager is not in itself preferable to that of the polite Londoner. The real value of the language of the *Lyrical Ballads* is not that it is the speech of 'the lower and middle classes of society,' but that it is universal language of the heart in permanent and universal English words.

2. *Syntax*.

When we turn from the study of words *per se* to their logical relation to each other in the sentence—i. e., the syntax, we find that the combined influence of the *Reliques* and of Wordsworth's new principles had a much more distinct, and possibly a deleterious, influence upon his poetic

---

[1] Cf. *Memoirs* 1. 129.

[2] Of *Simon Lee* Wordsworth says: 'The expression when the hounds were out, "I dearly love their voices" [*Simon Lee* 48] was word for word' from the lips of the old man who served as the model for the superannuated huntsman [*Memoirs* 1. 111]. The beautiful lines in *The Solitary Reaper*,

> The music in my heart I bore
> Long after it was heard no more,

are almost word for word from the journal of Wordsworth's Quaker friend, Thomas Wilkinson. See the passage from the journal, quoted in Harper's *William Wordsworth* 2. 66.

style. He was indeed successful in discovering a vocabulary common to the speech of the peasant and that of the scholar—to elder poetry and modern conversation; and this vocabulary he used with precision. Accordingly, there was comparatively little for him to reject in the words employed in the *Lyrical Ballads;* they formed a nucleus for a larger and richer and more expressive poetic diction. With syntax it was not so. In endeavoring to imitate the intellectual processes of the simple mind, he lost sight of the natural and logical relations of thought to thought, usually expressed by syntax, and the necessity of preserving these relations in any adequate expression.

As Coleridge said[1]: 'We do not adopt the language of a class by the mere adoption of such words exclusively, as that class would use, or at least understand; but likewise by following the *order,* in which the words of such men are wont to succeed each other. Now this order, in the intercourse of uneducated men, is distinguished from the diction of their superiors in knowledge and power, by the greater *disjunction* and *separation* in the component parts of that, whatever it may be, which they wish to communicate. There is a want of that prospectiveness of mind, that *surview,* which enables a man to foresee the whole of what he is to convey, appertaining to any one point; and by this means so to subordinate and arrange the different parts according to their relative importance, as to convey it at once, and as an organized whole.' The uneducated man does not look forward, and see the end of his speech beyond the beginning. He goes on adding thought to thought as they come, and connecting subordinate and co-ordinate ideas indifferently by 'and,' or leaving them wholly disconnected.[2] His emphasis is the emphasis of feeling alone,

[1] *B. L.* 2. 43-44.
[2] There is a good specimen of rustic syntax in the letter from an old servant quoted in Southey's *Lives of Uneducated Poets,* p. 2, in the passage: 'The last of my humble attempts . . . subscribe myself.'

and, as Wordsworth noticed, he expresses this emphasis simply by repeating the important idea again and again—not by any attempt to subordinate the less important things to it. The result is that his speech has exactly the qualities that Coleridge discovered in too much of Wordsworth's poetry—'prolixity, repetition, and an eddying instead of a progression of thought.'[1] Yet this emotional rather than intellectual syntax has its worth for the poet; and for one who had sought a greater flexibility in the imitation of classical Latin, the discovery of the possibilities of variety and expressiveness in his own native idiom was invaluable.

The result of reproducing the syntax of the unlearned was not unlike the result of imitating their vocabulary. As the words that Wordsworth uses are the words of Chaucer, so his syntax is the syntax of a still earlier period. What Kellner says[2] of the prose of Alfred exactly describes the construction of sentences in the *Lyrical Ballads:* 'Alfred changes his construction in consequence of every change going on in his mind, while in a modern author the flow of the ideas is checked by the ready pattern of the syntactical construction. . . . The syntax of older periods is natural, *naïf*—that is, it follows much more closely the drift of the ideas, of mental images; the diction, therefore, looks as if it were extemporised, as if written on the spur of the moment, while modern syntax, fettered by logic, is artificial, the result of literary tradition, and therefore, far from being a true mirror of what is going on in the mind.'[2] To follow more closely 'the drift of ideas, of mental images,' to make his language a true mirror of what is going on in the mind, especially of the manner in which we associate ideas in a state of excitement—this was the object of Wordsworth in some of the much derided mannerisms in the *Lyrical Ballads.* As he himself said, he always had 'a worthy purpose.'

[1] *B. L.* 2. 109.
[2] *Historical Outlines of English Syntax,* p. 9.

THE LYRICAL BALLADS 153

The effect of emotion (or lack of thought) on syntax is manifest in various types of sentences in the *Lyrical Ballads,* from the struggling attempt to relate subject to predicate to the unavailing effort to create structures at once complex and unified. Even the most simple sentence is an intellectual achievement. The fusing of the ideas of subject and predicate in one organic whole often presents an almost insuperable difficulty to the uncultivated or excited mind. This is illustrated in one of the most frequent mannerisms of uneducated speech, which is also a special feature of the style of the popular ballads. When it occurs in literature, it is often copied from them.

> The dynt *yt* was both sad and sar.[1]
>
> The yerlle of Fyffe, withowghten stryffe
> *He* bowynd hym over Sulway.[2]
>
> Then forthe Syr Cauline *he* was ledde.[3]
>
> And Scarlette *he* was flyinge afoote.[4]

The mind, in its interest in the subject, tends to lose sight of the predicate, and to cling to the image suggested by the substantive. In order to proceed, it has to take a fresh start, so to speak, with the pronoun representing the substantive, and so quickly pass to the verb. Examples of this syntactical peculiarity are very frequent in the *Lyrical Ballads,*[5] where it appears for the first time in Wordsworth's poetry.

> The eye *it* cannot chuse but see.[6]
>
> But the least motion which they made,
> *It* seemed a thrill of pleasure.[7]

---

[1] *Chevy Chase* 85.
[2] *The Battle of Otterbourne* 5-6.
[3] *Sir Cauline,* Part II 17.
[4] *Robin Hood and Guy of Gisborne* 57.
[5] There are thirty-two examples of it in the thirteen *Lyrical Ballads.*
[6] *Expostulation and Reply* 17.
[7] *Lines Written in Early Spring* 15-16.

> Your *limbs* they are alive.[1]
>
> The pony *he* is mild and good.[2]
>
> Shame on me, Sir! this lusty lamb,
> *He* makes my tears to flow.[3]
>
> The owlet in the moonlight air,
> *He* shouts from nobody knows where.[4]
>
> The doctor *he* has made him wait.[5]
>
> The babe I carry on my arm,
> *He* saves for me my precious soul.[6]
>
> Alas! alas! that look so wild,
> *It* never, never came from me.[7]

The peculiar mannerism of style here illustrated was one that Wordsworth took few pains to correct in the later editions of these poems. The lines 'His ancles, they are swoln and thick,'[8] become:

> His body, dwindled and awry,
> Rests upon ankles swoln and thick.

In the lines

> The owlet in the moonlight air
> He shouts from nobody knows where,[9]

he is omitted; and the line, 'And Susan she begins to fear,'[10] is changed to 'And Susan now begins to fear.' The line, 'Her face it was enough for me,'[11] is altered by punctua-

---

[1] *We Are Seven* 34.
[2] *The Idiot Boy* 313.
[3] *The Last of the Flock* 17-18.
[4] *The Idiot Boy* 3-4.
[5] *Ibid.* 175.
[6] *The Mad Mother* 47-48.
[7] *Ibid.* 87-88.
[8] *Simon Lee* 35.
[9] *The Idiot Boy* 4-5.
[10] *Ibid.* 187.
[11] *The Thorn* 200.

tion—'Her face! it was enough for me.' But otherwise these lines remain as they first stood through all Wordsworth's attempts to correct his poems.

In Wordsworth's conversion of the line, 'Her face it was enough for me,' to 'Her face! it was enough for me,' by simply changing the punctuation, another type of syntax closely related to the one just mentioned is illustrated. Here the substantive stands by itself, or is connected with the preceding statement, and the pronominal subject and its predicate follow as a kind of explanation of the emotion implied in the single word and the mark of exclamation. Though this type is sometimes distinguished from the other only by punctuation, it represents a somewhat different psychological process. The intense concentration of the mind on the subject and all it suggests is more frankly represented, and the break between this and what follows is complete. This type of syntax occurs much less frequently than the other in the *Lyrical Ballads*. The following are examples of it:

>   All day she spun in her poor dwelling,
>   And then her three hours work at night!
>   Alas! 'twas hardly worth the telling.[1]

>   And then the wind! in faith, it was
>   A wind full ten times over.[2]

>   But when the pony moved his legs,
>   Oh! then for the poor idiot boy!
>   For joy he cannot hold the bridle.[3]

The difficulty in joining the two members of the sentence, resulting, in these cases, from the interest that the mind takes in the subject to the exclusion of the predicate, may also be caused by a special interest in the predicate. In this case, also, there is an attempt to strengthen the relation

---

[1] *Goody Blake and Harry Gill* 25-27.
[2] *The Thorn* 190-191.
[3] *The Idiot Boy* 82-84.

between the two by reduplicating the subject. These two types of reduplication are thus illustrated and described by Kellner:

> *Your husband he* is gone to save far off,
> Whilst others come to make him lose at home.
> —*Shakespeare.*
>
> *She* early left her sleepless bed,
> The fairest maid of Teviotdale.
> —*Scott.*

'These instances illustrate two different psychological processes, and accordingly two different constructions. In the first case, the subject is foremost in the consciousness of the speaker, and the other idea connected with it, viz., the predicate, is dimmed for a moment, so that it takes the speaker some time to catch hold of it again. In the second case, the speaker is so much under the impression of what he is going *to predicate,* that he forgets for a moment to tell the person addressed what he is predicating about, and it takes some time until he finds out his mistake. In both cases there is a distinct pause between the two expressions for the same subject; in both cases the hearer has the impression that there is some emotion at work in the mind of the speaker. Both these circumstances make the expression a favorite figure of speech.'[1]

This second type of reduplication is also not uncommon in the *Lyrical Ballads*[2]:

---

[1] *Historical Outlines of English Syntax,* p. 40.
[2] Cf. the parody of *Peter Bell* by John Hamilton Reynolds which appeared in 1819, just before Wordsworth's own poem of that name. (It is one of the few parodies of Wordsworth which really reproduce the poet's mannerisms of syntax. The oft quoted parody by Horace Smith in *Rejected Addresses,* for instance, has not caught the poet's style at all.)

> Now I arise, and away we go,
> My little hobby-horse and me.

THE LYRICAL BALLADS

> Not higher than a two years' child,
> It stands erect, *this aged thorn*.[1]

> Oh me! ten thousand times I'd rather
> That *he* had died, that *cruel father!*[2]

> Alas! *'tis* very little, *all*
> Which they can do between them.[3]

A reduplication whose psychological cause is very similar occurs when the interest in the predicate temporarily obscures the object:

> Alas! I should have had *him* still,
> My *Johnny*, till my dying day.[4]

Sometimes, however, the reduplication is really due to a quick mental conversion of the subject into the object.

> Thy lips, I feel *them*, baby.[5]

> And this poor thorn they clasp *it* round.[6]

But these are only simple examples of constructions that occur in more complicated forms—forms which often come very near the line where the broken emotional syntax passes over into a more sustained intellectual structure. The suggestion of sustained thought immediately converts an apparent reduplication into a familiar literary device:

> Fond lovers, yet not quite hob nob,
> *They* lengthen out the tremulous sob.[7]

---

[1] *The Thorn* 5-6.
[2] *Ibid.* 142-143.
[3] *Simon Lee* 55-56.
[4] *The Idiot Boy* 245-246. Cf. Reynolds' *Peter Bell:*
> And gathered leeches are to *him*,
> To *Peter Bell*, like gathered flowers.
[5] *The Mad Mother* 33.
[6] *The Thorn* 17.
[7] *The Idiot Boy* 299-300.

> Even *he,* of cattle the most mild,
> The pony had his share.[1]

> *Him* whom she loves, her Idiot Boy.[2]

In these cases the pronoun seems to be used, not in a somewhat helpless and impulsive effort to keep hold of the subject, but with deliberate forethought. In the first quotation, 'fond lovers' is in intentional apposition with 'they'; in the two others, the pronoun seems to be used to point forward to the substantive, which is purposely withheld for a moment, instead of being parenthetically inserted on second thought. Such nice gradations suggest the more intellectual uses to which Wordsworth's practice in imitating the untaught cadence of extemporaneous speech could be put. In the end it gave him a fine and flexible instrument.

But if the mind in which feeling triumphs over thought has some difficulty in fusing the primary elements of a sentence into an organic whole, it waxes increasingly helpless as it attempts to relate the larger units thus formed. Often there is no such attempt. The simple units are merely placed side by side, as in a child's first reader: 'I have a cat. My cat is white. My cat eats rats.' This is a favorite method in the *Lyrical Ballads:*

> Her eyes are wild, her head is bare,
> The sun had burnt her coal-black hair;
> Her eyebrows have a rusty stain,
> And she came far from over the main.
> She has a baby on her arm.[3]

> I met a little cottage girl,
> She was eight years old, she said.[4]

> I have a boy of five years old,
> His face is fair and fresh to see;

---

[1] *The Idiot Boy* 250-251.
[2] *Ibid.* 16.
[3] *The Mad Mother* 1-5.
[4] *We Are Seven* 5-6.

> His limbs are cast in beauty's mould,
> And dearly he loves me.[1]

When the conjunctive *and* is used, it is inserted rather casually, as in ordinary speech, and does not connect the ideas in the series that are most closely related to each other.

Where every statement has exactly the same structure, there is, of course, no emphasis, no indication of proportion and relation. But this is generally expressed by the continual repetition, with changes and augmentations, of the fact uppermost in the mind of the speaker. Apart from the first group of philosophical poems, most of the *Lyrical Ballads* are wonderful complexes of such repetitions; the thoughts seem to be woven together, appearing and disappearing like the different colored threads in a carpet. Of this type of structure, *The Thorn* is the best example. In the first stanza, for instance, note how the two principal features of the thorn—its age and its erectness—are intertwined with a continually increasing number of illustrative details.

> There is a thorn; it looks so old,
> In truth you'd find it hard to say,
> How it could ever have been young,
> It looks so old and grey.
> Not higher than a two years' child,
> It stands erect this aged thorn;
> No leaves it has, no thorny points;
> It is a mass of knotted joints,
> A wretched thing forlorn.
> It stands erect, and like a stone
> With lichens it is overgrown.[2]

---

[1] *Anecdote for Fathers* 1-4. Cf. the use of an independent clause where we should expect a relative clause in the ballads, for example, *Edom O'Gordon* 85-86:

> Then bespake his dochter dear,
> She was baith jimp and sma.

[2] *The Thorn* 1-11.

A closer relation between the independent assertions is attempted in the parenthetical structure so frequent in conversation. Instead of employing subordinate clauses and modifying phrases, the details are inserted into the midst of other statements, just as they occur to the mind, each in the form of a complete little sentence:

> His head he raised—there was in sight,
> It caught his eye, he saw it plain—
> Upon the house-top, glittering bright,
> A broad and gilded vane.[1]

> Tis now some two and twenty years,
> Since she (her name is Martha Ray)
> Gave with a maiden's true good-will
> Her company to Stephen Hill.[2]

Sometimes, when a complex sentence is almost achieved, the subordinate clause has a tendency to detach itself and become independent, as in the following case:

> There's not a mother, no not one,
> But when she hears what you have done,
> Oh! Betty she'll be in a fright.[3]

In this sentence the logical relation of the separate parts might be expressed thus: 'There is not a mother who will not be in a fright when she hears what you have done.' But in his excitement, the speaker loses track of the relation of the last clause to the first, and lets it emerge into greater independence. The disposition to make each idea a separate assertion is also visible in the line,

> In Johnny's left-hand you may see
> The green bough's motionless and dead,[4]

---

[1] *Anecdote for Fathers* 49-52.
[2] *The Thorn* 115-118. Cf. *Chevy Chase* 89-90:
> 'Then bespake a squyar off Northombarlonde,
> Ric. Wytharynton was his nam,' etc.
[3] *The Idiot Boy* 24-26.
[4] *Ibid.* 88-89.

as compared with the more intellectual and literary construction to which Wordsworth altered it:

> In Johnny's left-hand you may see
> The green bough motionless and dead.

Sometimes, too, there is a connecting word used loosely to refer to an idea in the mind of the speaker not explicitly expressed:

> She talked and sung the woods among,
> And *it* was in the English tongue.[1]

Often relation is merely suggested rather than clearly indicated:

> Proud of herself, and proud of him,
> She sees him in his travelling trim;
> How quietly her Johnny goes.[2]

Even when a complex sentence is actually constructed, it is sometimes necessary to bind the parts together by a reduplication not unlike that employed in the joining of subject and predicate. As in the one case a pronoun was used to refer to the substantive, so in this an adverb, pointing back to the subordinate conjunction, is inserted in the principal clause:

> But when the ice our streams did fetter,
> Oh *then* how her old bones would shake.[3]

> Now, though he knows poor Johnny well,
> *Yet* for his life he cannot tell
> What he has got upon his back.[4]

But to list all the peculiarities of impulsive speech to be found in the *Lyrical Ballads* is impossible. We might speak of the flexible order of words—of inversions, not arbitrary

---

[1] *The Mad Mother* 9-10.
[2] *The Idiot Boy* 99-101.
[3] *Goody Blake and Harry Gill* 41-42.
[4] *The Idiot Boy* 124-126.

and unidiomatic, as in the descriptive poems, but natural and expressive; of the trick of repeating adjectives or adverbs[1]; or of repeating the noun with some added modifier[2]; of the use of a noun for an adjective ('His face was gloom; his heart was sorrow'),[3] etc.; but this would swell our study to unwieldy dimensions. Just because Wordsworth is trying to write as men talk—to register in the syntax all the shifting ideas and currents of emotion—it is very difficult to classify his constructions. They conform to no system. Each sentence is a living organism, as wayward and individual as other organisms in their undisciplined natural state.

In many cases the reader may wax impatient, and say with Coleridge[4]: 'It is indeed very possible to adopt in a poem the unmeaning repetitions, habitual phrases, and other blank counters, which an unfurnished or confused understanding interposes at short intervals, in order to keep hold of his subject, which is still slipping from him, and to give him time for recollection; or, in mere aid of vacancy, as in the scanty companies of a country stage the same player pops backwards and forwards, in order to prevent the appearance of empty spaces, in the procession of Macbeth, or Henry VIII. But what assistance to the poet, or ornament to the poem, these can supply, I am at a loss to conjecture.'

But this is one of the instances in which Coleridge's criticism is decidedly peevish. Whatever might have been the absolute value of these tricks of speech, as a preliminary inquiry into the sources of literary style, an experiment

---

[1] *Goody Blake and Harry Gill* 101; *Anecdote for Fathers* 12, 57; *The Thorn* 5. 4; *The Idiot Boy* 96; etc. Such repetition is characteristic of the ballads; cf. *Sir Aldingar* 147: 'Then woeful, woeful was her hart.'

[2] *The Mad Mother* 27-28; *The Idiot Boy* 28-29; *The Complaint of the Forsaken Indian Woman* 36, etc.

[3] Cf. *The Idiot Boy* 254: 'Tis silence all on every side.'

[4] *B. L.* 2. 43.

in basing literary form upon the actual psychology of speech, they were far from worthless. The thoroughness and honesty of the experiment were sufficient to make it of value, merely as a scientific study; the fact that some of the *Lyrical Ballads* were never superseded in popular affection by the poet's greater and more elaborate efforts shows that it was also an artistic achievement—that the language was not the language of a class alone, but of the general heart of man.

3. *Narrative and Lyrical Technique.*

In attempting to make the language of the lower and middle classes the medium of poetry, Wordsworth rejected the devices usually employed in the eighteenth century to raise poetry above prose. Personification and periphrasis do not occur in the *Lyrical Ballads*. But, for the outworn arts of heroic poetry, he substituted the no less obvious arts of the popular ballad, interpreting and modifying them in the light of his own observations of rustic psychology. The two devices most frequently employed are the personal appeal to the reader—sometimes by the use of the second person, more often by an assertion of the writer's veracity, or a statement of the source of his information—and the use of repetition, sometimes in the form of a refrain.

In employing the first device, Wordsworth went far beyond his models, and thereby developed one of the most clumsy and ineffective mannerisms of his style—a mannerism which clung to him long after his experiments in rustic syntax had developed into a flexible and elaborate medium of thought, as well as feeling. The exchange of the impersonal tone of his poems hitherto for these garrulous intrusions of the speaker into the course of the story was a disadvantage rather than an advantage. However, these numerous tags are not unsuitable in the highly colloquial language of the ballads:

> Two poor old dames, as *I have known*.[1]
>
> There's no one knows, as *I have said*.[2]
>
> His hunting feats have him bereft
> Of his right eye, as *you may see*.[3]
>
> Yet never had she, well or sick,
> As *every man who knew her says*,
> A pile beforehand, wood or stick.[4]

These and the like are obviously paralleled, not only in the habits of rustic story-tellers, but by the narrative devices of the ballads:

> The sworde was scharpe and sore can byte,
> I *tell you in sertayne*.[5]
>
> I wis, if *you the trouthe would know*,
> There was many a weeping eye.[6]

But it is in the use of the ballad-repetition that Wordsworth sometimes fails most signally, but more often achieves his most original artistic success. This device of style is eloquently defended in a note to *The Thorn* in the volume of 1800[7]: 'There is a numerous class of readers who imagine that the same words cannot be repeated without tautology; This is a great error: virtual tautology is much oftener produced by different words when the meaning is exactly the same. Words, a Poet's words more particularly, ought to be weighed in the balance of feeling, and not measured by the space which they occupy upon paper. For the Reader cannot be too often reminded that Poetry is passion: it is the history or science of feelings. Now every man must

---

[1] *Goody Blake and Harry Gill* 34.
[2] *The Thorn* 162.
[3] *Simon Lee* 26.
[4] *Goody Blake and Harry Gill* 53-55.
[5] *The Battle of Otterbourne* 109-110.
[6] *The Rising in the North* 51-52.
[7] Reprinted in the Oxford edition, pp. 899-900.

know that an attempt is rarely made to communicate impassioned feelings without something of an accompanying consciousness of the inadequateness of our own powers, or the deficiencies of language. During such efforts there will be a craving in the mind, and as long as it is unsatisfied the Speaker will cling to the same words, or words of the same character. There are also various other reasons why repetition and apparent tautology are frequently beauties of the highest kind. Among the chief of these reasons is the interest which the mind attaches to words, not only as symbols of the passion, but as *things,* active and efficient, which are of themselves part of the passion. And further, from a spirit of fondness, exultation, and gratitude, the mind luxuriates in the repetition of words which appear successfully to communicate its feelings.'

The strength and the weakness of this position are both illustrated in the *Lyrical Ballads.* Wordsworth did not accurately distinguish between the cases where language is really inadequate to express feeling—where a normal human mind is helpless under an abnormal emotion—and the cases in which the inadequacy is due only to the very elementary powers of sustained thought or expression in the persons whose psychological processes he chose to imitate. In this instance, he forgot to apply the principle that he himself found so fruitful—the principle that all figures of speech must be *justified by passion.* In such poems as *The Last of the Flock, The Mad Mother,* and *The Complaint of the Forsaken Indian Woman,* there is the justifying passion; and the recurring refrains are felt to be as artistically effective as they are true to the feeling to be expressed. But too often the outward form exists without a sufficient emotional or artistic reason for it, as will be seen. But even where the repetition does not have its source in emotion, it is a legitimate mode of emphasis, provided that it supplements, instead of supplanting, the emphasis that a proper selection and subordination of details can give. Such an emphasis really exists in the *Reliques*. The theme of the story is generally so momentous, so melodramatic (being usually the danger of violent death to some person or group of persons), and the outstanding circumstances so important, that the poet must necessarily omit minor details. In the naïve and rapid narrative, the repetition gives a reality to details that the hurried feelings of the reader would neglect, or serves to emphasize some really important situation. But in the majority of Wordsworth's ballads the swiftness of movement is lacking, and the slow and thoughtful reading that he demands often makes the repetition unnecessary as a matter of narrative technique. An analysis of the various uses to which Wordsworth has put the ballad-repetition will make this clearer.

In the group of the philosophical poems, this device is almost the only feature that Wordsworth's thoughtful verse has in common with his naïve models. The original pattern of such stanzas as the following is obvious:

> Why, William, on that old grey stone,
> Thus for the length of half a day,
> Why, William, sit you thus alone,
> And dream your time away?[1]

> Up! up! my friend and clear your looks,
> Why all this toil and trouble?
> Up! up! my friend, and quit your books,
> Or surely you'll grow double.[2]

These at once recall the familiar structure of the ballads:

> Here take her, Child of Elle, he sayd,
> And gave her lillye white hand;
> Here take my dear and only child,
> And with her half my land.[3]

---
[1] *Expostulation and Reply* 1-4.
[2] *The Tables Turned* 1-4.
[3] *The Child of Elle* 189-192.

In the philosophical poems the repetition of a stanza with slight variation, so familiar in the ballads, is skilfully employed to round out the thought, and point the moral. In *Expostulation and Reply* the poem ends with a reference to the words with which it began:

> Then ask not wherefore, here, alone,
>   Conversing as I may,
> I sit upon this old grey stone,
>   And dream my time away.

In the *Tables Turned* the thought rather than the words is repeated:

> Enough of science and of art;
>   Close up those barren leaves;
> Come forth and bring with you a heart
>   That watches and receives.

In the other philosophical poems there is a similar repetition:

> Edward will come with you, and pray
>   Put on with speed your woodland dress,
> And bring no book, for this one day
>   We'll give to idleness,[1]

is echoed in the lines,

> Then come, my sister! come, I pray,
>   With speed put on your woodland dress,
> And bring no book; for this one day
>   We'll give to idleness.[2]

The words,

> To her fair works did nature link
>   The human soul that through me ran;
> And much it griev'd my heart to think
>   What man has made of man,[3]

[1] *To my Sister* 13-16.
[2] *Ibid.* 37-40.
[3] *Lines Written in Early Spring* 5-8.

are recalled in the stanza,

> If I these thoughts may not prevent,
> If such be of my creed the plan,
> Have I not reason to lament
> What man has made of man?[1]

Here it will be seen that the closing of the poem with a recurrence to the thought with which it began, or which forms the centre of it, is an effective means of securing unity, and of emphasizing the theme.

In the narrative poems the repetition is more frequent, and possibly less justifiable. In *We are Seven* the repetition of the words which form the title, with various modifications—'Seven in all,' 'Seven are we,' 'Yet you are seven,' 'Seven boys and girls are we,' 'O Master, we are seven,' 'Nay, we are seven'—is the repetition of the one essential thought in the poem, and represents the obstinate clinging of the child's mind to one idea: and hence it is effective. In *Goody Blake and Harry Gill* there is a similar effort to emphasize the theme, or rather the climax of the story by repetition:

> That evermore his teeth they chatter,
> Chatter, chatter, chatter, still.

In *The Anecdote for Fathers* this is hardly the case. Here, where the poet is speaking in his own person, and is not reiterating an important idea, the repetitious character of the narrative portion simply shows a difficulty in getting on—an unnecessary eddying of thought about something that should not hold it so long:

> 'My little boy, which like you more,'
> I said, and took him by the arm—
> 'Our home by Kilve's delightful shore,
> Or here at Liswyn farm?'

[1] *Lines Written in Early Spring* 21-24.

> 'And tell me, had you rather be,'
> I said, and held him by the arm,
> 'At Kilve's smooth shore by the green sea,
> Or here at Liswyn farm?'[1]

Here it is obvious that the second stanza really adds nothing to the first—as Wordsworth recognized after Coleridge had used this passage as an example of the tendency to eddy rather than to progress. In later editions he omitted the first stanza, to the great improvement of the poem.

But it is in the lyrical poems, where the repetition becomes a refrain, that Wordsworth's attempt to make literary artifice an accurate reflection of psychological processes is most successful. Like other poetical devices, the refrain has its origin in a characteristic of impassioned feeling. The mind under the influence of a great emotion is intensely preoccupied with a single idea, or group of associated ideas. Around these all other ideas tend to circle; in this every train of thought begins and ends. When a new and alien series of images is suggested, the mind follows it but a little way, and then finds some means of linking it with the single overwhelming feeling. Generally, as Wordsworth noticed, the idea is repeated again and again in the same or very similar words. But in many songs there is no effort whatever to trace the process by which the mind returns to the refrain. It is merely added every time at the end of a stanza or set number of verses, whether it has any real connection with them or not.

To make a natural, rather than an artificial, use of this device is the aim of Wordsworth in all the poems we have grouped as lyrics. Of these, *The Thorn* seems the least effective. This is partly due to the intrusion of the shadowy speaker, who is neither an old skipper nor the poet himself, but something between, and who, moreover, is not telling his own story. The lyrical element is thus partly dissipated

---

[1] *Anecdote for Fathers* 29-36.

before it pierces through the somewhat alien medium to the imagination of the reader. Nevertheless, in introducing the refrain,

>Oh misery! Oh misery!
>Oh woe to me! O misery!

Wordsworth has represented it as a natural result of the tendency of the adhesive mind of the old seaman to cling to the idea that has impressed him, and to repeat it in the same words—as well as an expression of the feeling of the poor woman.

In *The Last of the Flock* there is a double refrain which is much more skilfully used. The speaker naturally begins with the explanation,

>Shame on me, Sir! this lusty lamb,
>He makes my tears to flow.
>To-day I fetched him from the rock;
>*He is the last of all my flock,*

which suggests the history of the flock. When he comes to the account of his fifty comely sheep, the contrast between the memory of these and the one last lamb in his arms suddenly forces itself upon him, and he recurs to his first thought, but expresses the thought in different words:

>*This lusty lamb of all my store*
>*Is all that is alive:*

adding,

>And now I care not if we die
>And perish all of poverty.

This last reflection immediately suggests the rest of his story, and he begins again. He had to sell his flock one by one to buy his little children bread, he says. As he speaks, the woefulness of this takes possession of his mind; and, accordingly, every added group of details naturally ends in the reflection, 'For me it was a woeful day,' which becomes the refrain:

> To see it melt like snow away,
> For me it was a woeful day.
>
> They dwindled one by one away;
> For me it was a woeful day.

And from the elaboration of this thought of the dwindling, the mind is brought back to the original refrain, and the poem ends in the thought with which it began:

> They dwindled, Sir, sad sight to see!
> From ten to five, from five to three,
> A lamb, a weather, and a ewe;
> And then at last, from three to two;
> And of my fifty, yesterday
> I had but only one,
> And here it lies upon my arm,
> Alas! and I have none;
> To-day I fetched it from the rock;
> *It is the last of all my flock.*

In the *Complaint of the Forsaken Indian Woman,* there is a very lovely use of a double refrain. Each refrain seems to suggest the other, and, as in *The Last of the Flock,* both are united at the end; and the effect is still further increased by an echoing of the rhymes of the refrain through the rest of the poem:

> Before I see another day,
> Oh let my body die away!
>
> Then here contented will I lie;
> Alone I could not fear to die;

both of which are again suggested in the words:

> For strong and without pain I lay,
> My friends, when ye were gone away.
>
> Too soon, my friends, ye went away,
> For I had many things to say,
>
> All stiff with ice the ashes lie;
> And they are dead, and I will die,

> For-ever left alone am I,
> Then wherefore should I fear to die?

In the last lines the two refrains unite:

> My poor forsaken child! if I
> For once could have thee close to me,
> With happy heart I then should die,
> And my last thoughts would happy be.
> I feel my body die away,
> I shall not see another day.

Here certainly the eddying of thought is used with wonderful artistic effect, as subtle as it is beautiful and pathetic.

In *The Mad Mother* the repetition is still more delicate. It is used chiefly in a remarkable complex of rhymes, which repeat and echo each other. The result is a curious haunting cadence. Every rhyme falls on the ear like a refrain, though few are aware in what this refrain-like quality consists.

To trace further Wordsworth's use of the real language of men, and the psychological processes behind it, is perhaps unnecessary. A large book could be written on his use of repetition alone; but the discussion of each single example of every different usage would be more laborious than edifying. From the examples already cited it is evident that the language of the *Lyrical Ballads* is as much the result of conscious art as the language of *Paradise Lost*. It was a deliberate and thorough application of a theory which seemed strange enough to 'indolent reviewers,' but which has much in common with the theory at the basis of the more scientific study of language for the last century.[1]

---

[1] Cf. Kellner, *Historical Outlines of English Syntax*, p. 10. 'In the study of English syntax, the vulgar talk cannot be overlooked, nay—but for the difficulty of getting trustworthy materials—we ought, in discussing the evolution of syntax, to start from the rustic talk, just as a botanist, in dealing with the evolution of the strawberry, will not take the artificial fruit, but the wild strawberry of the wood as the starting-point of his study.'

Of course, in his experiment, Wordsworth made some artistic mistakes, and fell into several bad habits. A man of twenty-eight, 'not much used to composition,' is not likely to produce poetry uniformly excellent in workmanship. He is the less likely to do so when he has the misfortune to be born in a bad age, and must rediscover poetic principles and models for himself.

Among the evil results of the experiment was the unnecessary use of the various tags—'why should I fear to say?' etc.—which occasionally fill half a line with nothing at all; and the loss of that energetic forward movement so characteristic of his descriptive poems. The eddying repetitious narrative of the untrained speaker has its emotional uses; but it is not an ideal standard. The effect of a poem should result, as far as possible, from its inner structure. Where there is a continual necessity for external bolsters—repetitions and appeals to the reader—art in its highest sense does not exist. There is not a skilful adaptation of means to the attainment of a desired end.

Of this high impersonal art, where the means are concealed like the bony structure of a living organism, instead of shamelessly flaunted, Wordsworth was to give many examples. Indeed there are some examples of it in the *Lyrical Ballads*—in *The Complaint of the Forsaken Indian Woman* and *The Mad Mother,* for instance; generally the art in this collection of poems is not so obvious as it seems. But over against the triumphs we may place such a failure in structure as the original *Simon Lee,* on which Wordsworth's own alterations were the best possible criticism.

In *Simon Lee* the poet is speaking in his own character, not that of a peasant or the garrulous old skipper in *The Thorn;* but he is nearly as helpless to mass details, and entirely to finish one thought before he proceeds to the next. The following is the order in which the details of Simon's appearance were first given:—ancient hunting feats—*one eye left*—*a cheek like a cherry*—loss of his master and friends—*one eye left*—*disabled limbs*—loss of kindred—his wife—*disabled limbs*—present attempts at agriculture—ancient hunting feats—his wife—his present attempts at agriculture—his *disabled limbs*. Here it is apparent that there is no control over the details, no attempt to group them at all; the mind of the poet circles round and round among them—advancing a little in the process, to be sure, but not in the fashion of a well disciplined intellect. It will also be seen that in the nature of the case there is nothing to produce his apparent helplessness—no difficulty in the simple facts, no passion to disorganize the mind. It was simply a bad habit into which his attempt to imitate the methods of untrained speakers had led him. This he himself later realized. After numerous and perplexing changes, the poem assumed its present form, in which 'the traits and evidences of Simon's early vigour are concentred within stanzas I-III, while those of his sad decline are brought together in stanzas IV-VII, the contrast being marked by the phrase, "But oh, the heavy change!" '[1]; and a reasonable order is substituted for the chaos of the first edition.

Similar changes were introduced into *The Thorn*. Of course in this poem there is more reason for the repetition, because the writer is speaking in the character of a talkative old seaman, whose mind is overwhelmed by a terrible, tragic story. But even here Wordsworth later saw that he had gone too far, and omitted several wholly unnecessary and repetitious stanzas, without altering the impression which he wished to convey. As they stand in the Oxford edition, *Simon Lee* and *The Thorn* are perhaps more really typical of Wordsworth's best art in 1798 than they were in the form which they first assumed. He has pruned the excrescences without destroying the essential character.

But a still better criticism of the style of the *Lyrical Ballads* is to be found in the second volume of poems added

[1] *Lyrical Ballads*, ed. Hutchinson, note on *Simon Lee*.

to the *Lyrical Ballads* in 1800—the 'Other Poems' mentioned in the title. In the *Preface* the phrase 'language of conversation in the lower and middle classes of society,' has become the 'real language of men in a state of vivid sensation.' And this more general application corresponds to a distinct change in the style. It has become the real language of men—of a typical man speaking—and not the language of a class. The peculiarities noted in the earlier poems have for the most part entirely disappeared. For the repetition, the uneducated syntax, the extremely bald vocabulary of the first ballads, there has been substituted the tone of cultivated conversation, easy, flexible, straightforward, controlling the passion and the details, not controlled by them. The medium of communication between the poet and the reader is no longer the rustic, or a modern imitation of an ancient minstrel; it is a quiet, intelligent, sympathetic observer, who passes on what he has seen to an equally intelligent and sympathetic reader, in language unadorned, but perfectly adequate.

This conversational tone, with its self-control, and its unconstrained and progressive structure of the sentences and paragraphs, may be illustrated by endless comparisons. The extremes of the two styles may be seen in the first stanza of *The Thorn,* already quoted, as compared with the beginning of *Michael:*

> *If* from the public way you turn your steps
> Up the tumultuous brook of Green-head Gill,
> You will suppose that with an upright path
> Your feet must struggle; in *such* bold ascent
> The pastoral Mountains front you, face to face.
> *But,* courage! *for* beside *that* boisterous Brook
> The mountains have all open'd out themselves,
> And made a hidden valley of their own.
> No habitation there is seen; but such
> As journey thither find themselves alone
> With a few sheep, with rocks and stones, and kites
> That overhead are sailing in the sky.

Here, despite a few polysyllabic words, like *tumultuous, habitation,* etc., the vocabulary is not essentially changed; but how different is what Coleridge calls the *ordonnance* of the style—the various and expressive syntax! In the first stanza of *The Thorn* there are practically no conjunctions; no type of sentence is employed save the simplest independent clauses set side by side. Where subordination and relation are implied, they are not expressed, as in the lines,[1]

>   it looks so old,
>   In truth you'd find it hard to say
>   How it could ever have been young,
>   It looks so old and gray,

where the prose expression would be: 'It looks so old and gray that in truth you would find it hard to tell how it could ever have been young.' The omission of the conjunction *that,* and the repetition of 'it looks so old and gray,' give the characteristic eddying movement to the verse, and a certain helplessness to the syntax. But in *Michael* there is no such difficulty. All the necessary connecting tissue of conjunctions and demonstratives is here; and there is a steady onward movement, with no repetition, no picking up of dropped stitches—so to speak. The poet still 'talks' to the reader; there is the tone, the manner, of spoken language in the use of the second person, and in such an expression as 'But courage!' etc.; but the speaker is no longer an excited rustic who finds his language slightly inadequate to the occasion, and cannot keep everything in his mind at once. He is the spectator *ab extra,* calmly though sympathetically holding all the details in his mind in their proper relation to each other, and setting them before the hearer steadily, and without haste.

A similar improvement in the character of the more lyrical style is to be discovered in the beautiful fragment,

---

[1] *The Thorn* 1-4.

The Danish Boy, which employs a stanza almost exactly like that of *The Thorn,* and makes a similar attempt to give a romantic association to a particular spot by connecting it with a half visionary figure:

> Between two sister moorland rills
> There is a spot that seems to lie
> Sacred to flowerets of the hills,
> And sacred to the sky.
> And in this smooth and open dell
> There is a tempest-stricken tree;
> A corner-stone by lightning cut,
> The last stone of a cottage-hut;
> And in this dell you see
> A thing no storm can e'er destroy,
> The shadow of a Danish Boy.[1]

But this does not mean that Wordsworth has abandoned his first attempt to make syntax follow more accurately the movement of thought. He has merely learned that the effect of extemporaneous speech may be conveyed without an absolutely literal imitation of all its repetitions and ineptitudes. In *The Brothers,* for instance, the characteristics of the syntax of the *Lyrical Ballads* are retained, with further improvements and variations; but at the same time there is greater skill in the arrangement of details, and a real distinction of style.

The opening is a model of exposition:

> These Tourists, Heaven preserve us! needs must live
> A profitable life: some glance along
> Rapid and gay, as if the earth were air,
> And they were butterflies to wheel about
> Long as their summer lasted; some, as wise
> Upon the forehead of a jutting crag
> Sit perch'd with book and pencil on their knee,
> And look and scribble, scribble on and look,
> Until a man might travel twelve stout miles,
> Or reap an acre of his neighbor's corn.
> But, for that moping son of Idleness
> Why can he tarry *yonder?*

[1] *The Danish Boy* 1-11.

Here the method of procedure from the genèral to the particular could hardly be bettered. There is the statement concerning the character of tourists in general; the division of the genus into species; and then the reference to the particular individual who stands by himself. The sentence-structure, too, is varied and flexible; yet the tone of conversation is maintained throughout, and the vocabulary is strictly the vocabulary of ordinary speech. Of course, when the old vicar begins to tell his story, he falls into the peculiarities of speech which we are wont to call ungrammatical; but the progressive movement is not lost. The expressiveness of the deviations from standard syntax, marked by italics, will be noticed at once, as well as a fine antique quality in the language, which reminded Lamb of Shakespeare:

>That's Walter Ewbank.
>He had as white a head and fresh a cheek
>As ever were produc'd by youth and age
>Engendering in the blood of hale fourscore.
>For five long generations had the heart
>Of Walter's forefathers o'erflow'd the bounds
>Of their inheritance, that single cottage,
>*You see it yonder,* and those few green fields.
>They toil'd and wrought, and still, from sire to son,
>Each struggled, and each yielded as before
>A little—yet a little—and *old Walter,*
>*They left* to him the family heart, and land
>With other burthens than the crop it bore.
>Year after year the old man still preserv'd
>A chearful mind, *and buffeted* with bond,
>Interest and mortgages; at last he sank,
>And went into his grave before his time.
>Poor Walter! *whether it was care that spurr'd him*
>*God only knows,* but to the very last,
>He had the lightest foot in Ennerdale.[1]

As *The Brothers* is the best example of the real language of men attempted in the volume of 1798, so *Ruth* is a

---

[1] *The Brothers* 200-219.

happier example of the use of the mannerisms adopted from the ballads than anything in the first edition. Here all the old tricks reappear; but they have become minor elements in a far more elaborate and finished technique.

For the original simplicity of syntax there is substituted a structure more complex and sustained. Now and then, to be sure, Wordsworth retains the method of simply setting more or less naturally related facts side by side, in the form of independent statements, without an attempt to show their natural relations, as in the stanza,

> There came a Youth from Georgia's shore,
> A military Casque he wore
> With splendid feathers drest;
> He brought them from the Cherokees;
> The feathers nodded in the breeze
> And made a gallant crest,[1]

where the relations of thought to thought might be expressed in somewhat this fashion—'There came a youth from Georgia's shore, *who* wore a military casque dressed with splendid feathers, *which* he brought from the Cherokees. *These* feathers nodded in the breeze.' But for the most part there is sufficient connecting tissue, and the light and shade and emphasis are furnished by proper subordination. When this is lacking, the reader, perceiving how well the poet knows his trade, is inclined to think that there is some reason for the omission—a peculiar emphasis to be gained thereby. But for one stanza of this type there are a dozen in which all the resources of elaborate and varied syntax seem to be at the writer's command. The greater part of *Ruth* is a model of perspicuous sentence-structure. Moreover, the various narrative-tags are no longer obtrusive, though they still occur:

---

[1] *Ruth* 12-18. (The references are to the first version of *Ruth*, in the *Lyrical Ballads* of 1800.)

> But, as *you have before been told*
> This Stripling, sportive, gay and bold,
> . . . . .
>
> Had roamed about with vagrant bands
> Of Indians in the west.[1]
>
> Even so they did; and *I may say*
> That to sweet Ruth that happy day
> Was more than human life.[2]
>
> A Barn her *winter* bed supplies,
> But till the warmth of summer skies
> And summer days is gone,
> (And in *this tale we all agree*)
> She sleeps beneath the greenwood tree,
> And other home hath none.[3]

They are merged in the general excellence of the style, and seem a natural part of it.

Again, there is something peculiarly effective in the occasional use of the ballad-repetition,

> Ere she had wept, ere she had mourned,
> A young and happy child,[4]

and the naïve, ballad-like, ending is very beautiful:

> Farewel! and when thy days are told
> Ill-fated Ruth! in hallowed mould
> Thy corpse shall buried be,
> For thee a funeral bell shall ring,
> And all the congregation sing
> A Christian psalm for thee.[5]

[1] *Ruth* 109-110, 113-14.
[2] *Ibid.* 100-102.
[3] *Ibid.* 199-204.
[4] *Ibid.* 221-222. Cf. *The Child of Elle* 169-170:

> Fair Emmeline sighed, fair Emmeline wept,
> And all did trembling stand.

[5] *Ibid.* 223-228.

Hence, as early as 1800, Wordsworth was already outgrowing the Advertisement to the *Lyrical Ballads,* and with it the experimental period of his career. Some traces of the original theory of course remain, both in the hard bits of literal, matter-of-fact statement in poems like *Alice Fell,* and in his occasional defense of so-called 'prosaic' language. Certainly the original theory continued to interest him until about 1805, the last reprinting of the *Lyrical Ballads* of 1800 with their preface. But for the real source of his poetic diction henceforth we must look mainly to his reading. In the volumes of 1807 the influence of Spenser and of the Elizabethan library furnished by Lamb is everywhere evident, especially the pure and quiet cadences of the later Elizabethans, Daniel, Drayton, and Beaumont. The sonnets, which form so numerous and so beautiful a part of his poetry after 1800, were written under the immediate influence of Milton. The noble and unique language of the *Prelude* is created out of the apparently unpromising terminology of the philosophers, Hartley and Darwin. No doubt the eloquent discourses of Coleridge served as an intermediary step in this alchemic transmutation. The poetry of 1814-1816 was influenced by the re-reading of Virgil and other Latin authors. There is a pensive Virgilian graciousness of language in some of his too much neglected later poems, such as the *Egyptian Maid.* The language of the later poems also reflects the stiff, but often deeply pathetic, Latin of early ecclesiastical literature. From sources like these, not from the speech of the dalesmen, was the greater part of Wordsworth's phraseology ultimately derived.

But, after all, it was the theory suggested in the Advertisement which taught Wordsworth to make this use of books. Through his apparent repudiation of the language of books he entered into his literary inheritance. His theory of poetic diction served as a test by which he might seek out the genuine metal of poetry, and appropriate it to himself. He had already shown a disposition to test and appropriate in his use of borrowed phrases in the *Descriptive Sketches*. But the touchstone, while good as far as it went, had not been sufficient. He had learned to judge natural imagery used in poetry in accordance with his own experience, and to include in his own work the expressions which satisfied him. But he had not learned to judge of language and the psychology of human expression. He merely took what pleased him, and what pleased him was the strange, the original, the fantastic. He had no social consciousness—no knowledge of the way in which others might react to the words that he used. The theory of the *Lyrical Ballads* awakened in him this social consciousness. He wished to learn how living men spoke, how they had always spoken. He learned to test his language in accordance both with general usage and with actual psychology. This gave him a control over the resources of his own tongue such as only the scholarly poets may have. After 1798 it is almost impossible to catch Wordsworth in a questionable use of a word or a slip of grammar. His vocabulary has a purity and precision which neither Milton nor Tennyson, the self-conscious artists in language, can equal—however they may surpass him in splendor and sonorous music. His sentence-structure is remarkable alike for its peculiar flexibility and for its strict observance of grammar and idiom. He continues to read more and more in the field of English literature, but with discrimination; at any moment he is ready to give an account of the literary faith that is in him. He had rediscovered the principles of English poetry, and in so doing had discovered himself. It is in this discovery, not in any experimental imitation of the speech of Tom, Dick, or Harry, that the true significance of Wordsworth's theory of poetic diction lies.

BIBLIOGRAPHY

The following bibliography contains only the titles of books to which a specific reference is made in the text:

Addison, Joseph. Criticisms of Paradise Lost (ed. Cook). Boston, 1892.
Bagehot, Walter. Literary Studies. London, 1879.
Blair, Hugh. Essays on Rhetoric. London, 1787.
Bowles, William L. Sonnets, written chiefly on Picturesque Spots, during a Tour. Bath, 1789.
Cicero, Marcus Tullius. De Oratore (ed. Wilkins). Oxford, 1879-92.
Cicero, Marcus Tullius. Oratory and Orators (tr. Watson). London, 1889.
Coleridge, Samuel Taylor. Biographia Epistolaris (ed. Turnbull). London, 1911.
Coleridge, Samuel Taylor. Biographia Literaria (ed. Shawcross). Oxford, 1907.
Coleridge, Samuel Taylor. Complete Poetical Works (ed. E. H. Coleridge). Oxford, 1912.
Coleridge, Samuel Taylor. Letters (ed. E. H. Coleridge). Boston, 1895.
Coleridge, Sara. Memoir and Letters (ed. by her daughter). New York, 1874.
Cook, Albert S. The Art of Poetry. Boston, 1892.
Cooper, Lane. A Concordance to the Poems of William Wordsworth. London, 1911.
Cowper, William. Works (ed. Southey). London, 1836-37.
Darwin, Erasmus. Zoönomia. London, 1801.
Darwin, Erasmus. The Botanic Garden. London, 1791.
Dennis, John. The Grounds of Criticism in Poetry. London, 1704.
De Vere, Aubrey. Essays, chiefly on Poetry. London, 1887.
De Vere, Aubrey. Essays, chiefly Literary and Ethical. London, 1889.
Dryden, John. Essays (ed. Ker). Oxford, 1900.
Dryden, John. Works (ed. Scott-Saintsbury). Edinburgh, 1882-93.
Goldsmith, Oliver. Works (ed. Gibbs). London, 1885.
Gray, Thomas. Letters (ed. Tovey). London, 1900.
Hamelius, Paul. Die Kritik in der Englischen Literatur des 17. und 18. Jahrhunderts. Leipzig, 1897.
Harper, George MacLean. William Wordsworth. New York, 1916.
Hartley, David. Observations on Man. London, 1810.

HAZLITT, WILLIAM. Literary Remains. London, 1836.
HORACE QUINTUS FLACCUS. Ars Poetica. (Art of Poetry, ed. Cook.) Boston, 1892.
HUTTON, RICHARD HOLT. Essays, Theological and Literary. London, 1888.
JOHNSON, SAMUEL. Lives of the English Poets (ed. Hill). Oxford, 1905.
JONSON, BEN. Timber (ed. Shelling). Boston, 1892.
KELLNER, LEON. Historical Outlines of English Syntax. London and New York, 1892.
PETIT DE JULLEVILLE. Histoire de la Langue et de la Litterature Française des Origines a 1900. Paris, 1897.
LAMB, CHARLES. Works (ed. Lucas). London, 1903-1905.
LAMB, CHARLES. Letters (ed. Macdonald). London, 1903.
LEGOUIS, EMILE. The Early Life of William Wordsworth. New York, 1897.
LIENEMAN, KURT. Die Belesenheit von William Wordsworth. Weimar, 1908.
LUCAS, E. V. The Life of Charles Lamb. New York and London, 1905.
MOORE, J. L. Tudor-Stuart Views on the Growth, Status, and Destiny of the English Language. Halle, 1910.
POPE, ALEXANDER. Works (ed. Courthope and Elwin). London, 1871-89.
PRATT, ALICE E. The Use of Color in the Verse of the English Romantic Poets. Chicago, 1898.
QUINTILIAN, MARCUS FABIUS. Institutes of Oratory (tr. Watson). London, 1891-92.
REYNOLDS, MYRA. The Treatment of Nature in English Poetry between Pope and Wordsworth. Chicago, 1896.
ROBINSON, HENRY CRABB. Diary, Reminiscences, and Correspondence (ed. Sadler). Boston, 1869.
SCOTT, JOHN. Critical Essays on Some of the Poems of Several English Poets. London, 1785.
SHAIRP, JOHN C. Aspects of Poetry. Boston and New York, 1892.
SMITH, G. GREGORY. Elizabethan Critical Essays. Oxford, 1904.
SPENCE, JOSEPH. Anecdotes, Observations, and Characters of Books and Men. London, 1820.
SPINGARN, JOEL E. Critical Essays of the Sevententh Century. Oxford, 1908.
WARTON, JOSEPH. An Essay on the Genius and Writings of Pope. London, 1782.
WORDSWORTH, CHRISTOPHER. Memoirs of William Wordsworth (ed. Reed). Boston, 1851.

WORDSWORTH, CHRISTOPHER. Social Life at the English Universities in the Eighteenth Century. Cambridge, 1874.
WORDSWORTH, WILLIAM. Lyrical Ballads. Bristol, 1798. (In the possession of Mrs. Cynthia Morgan St. John.)
WORDSWORTH, WILLIAM. Lyrical Ballads. London, 1798.
WORDSWORTH, WILLIAM. Lyrical Ballads (ed. Hutchinson). London, 1798.
WORDSWORTH, WILLIAM. Lyrical Ballads, with other Poems. London, 1800.
WORDSWORTH, WILLIAM. Lyrical Ballads, with Pastoral and Other Poems. London, 1802.
WORDSWORTH, WILLIAM. Lyrical Ballads. Philadelphia, 1802.
WORDSWORTH, WILLIAM. Lyrical Ballads, with Pastoral and Other Poems. London, 1805.
WORDSWORTH, WILLIAM. Poems. London, 1807.
WORDSWORTH, WILLIAM. Poems including Lyrical Ballads and the Miscellaneous Pieces of the Author, with additional Poems, a new Preface and a Supplementary Essay. London, 1815.
WORDSWORTH, WILLIAM. Miscellaneous Poems. London, 1820.
WORDSWORTH, WILLIAM. Poetical Works. London, 1827.
WORDSWORTH, WILLIAM. Poetical Works. London, 1836.
WORDSWORTH, WILLIAM. Poetical Works. London, 1840-1.
WORDSWORTH, WILLIAM. Poems. London, 1845.
WORDSWORTH, WILLIAM. Poetical Works (ed. Knight), including a Life of Wordsworth. Edinburgh, 1882-89.
WORDSWORTH, WILLIAM. Poetical Works (ed. Dowden) with Memoir. London, 1892-93.
WORDSWORTH, WILLIAM. Poetical Works (ed. Hutchinson). London, New York, 1907.
Prose Writings of Wordsworth (ed. Knight). London, 1893.
Letters of the Wordsworth Family from 1787 to 1855 (ed. Knight). Boston and London, 1907.
Wordsworth's Prefaces and Essays on Poetry (ed. A. J. George). Boston, 1892.
Wordsworth's Literary Criticism (ed. Nowell C. Smith). London, 1905.
WORDSWORTH, WILLIAM. Poems and Extracts Chosen by William Wordsworth for an Album presented to Lady Mary Lowther, Christmas, 1819. London, 1905.
A Description of the Wordsworth and Coleridge Manuscripts in the possession of Mr. T. Norton Longman (ed. W. Hale White). London and New York, 1897.
Transactions of the Wordsworth Society. Edinburgh, 1882-87.

INDEX OF PROPER NAMES

Addison, 16, 39, 57, 58, 59, 61.
Alfred, 152.
Ariosto, 17, 111.
Aristotle, 7, 23, 58, 59, 129.
Arnold, Matthew, vii, 2, 6.
Ascham, 6, 7, 9.

Bagehot, xi, 2.
Beattie, 93.
Beaumont, John, 181.
Beaupuy, 111.
Bembo, 17.
Bernard of Clairveaux, 36.
Blair, 49.
Boileau, 22, 33, 34, 35, 55.
Boyer, 113.
Bowles, 85, 87, 88, 99, 114, 118, 119, 125.
Browne, Sir Thomas, 15, 22.
Burns, 3, 61, 94, 118, 119.
Bürger, 122, 123, 124.
Byron, 14.

Caesar, 7.
Campion, 15.
Catullus, 113.
Charles II, 4.
Chaucer, 2, 4, 10, 43, 112, 117, 139, 140, 144, 145, 148, 152.
Cheke, Sir John, 7.
Cicero, 7, 9, 11, 12, 113.
Coleridge, vii, viii, ix, x, xiv, 3, 4, 7, 13, 14, 16, 39, 52, 53, 62, 66, 67, 68, 85, 86, 99, 102, 104, 107, 108, 109, 110, 112, 113-140, 141, 144, 148, 151, 152, 162, 169, 176, 181.
Coleridge, Sara, xiv.
Collins, 62, 85, 87, 100, 115.
Cooper, Lane, xi.
Corneille, 23.
Cowley, 7, 16, 53.
Cowper, 3, 36, 39, 57, 61, 62, 88, 92, 94, 118.

Daniel, Samuel, 13, 15, 181.
Dante, 2.

Darwin, Erasmus, 102, 114, 115, 116, 118, 130, 181.
Delille, 93.
Demosthenes, 113.
Denham, 23.
Dennis, John, 52, 129.
DeQuincey, xiv.
DeVere, Aubrey, xi, xiv.
Donne, 7, 16.
Dowden, xi.
Drayton, 13, 14, 15, 181.
Dryden, xiv, 4, 6, 11, 13, 21-24, 26, 28-35, 39, 41, 42-45, 48, 49, 51, 52, 54, 57, 58, 60, 61, 74, 100, 112, 129.
Dyer, 63, 87, 99.

E. K., 5.
Elyot, Sir Thomas, 6.

Gardiner, Bishop, 6.
Gascoigne, 8, 20.
Gay, 40.
Gilbert, Sir Humphrey, 5.
Goldsmith, 3, 38, 54, 57, 58, 61.
Gray, 3, 54, 57, 60, 62, 92, 93, 100, 115.
Gunston, 46.

Hamilton, William Rowan, 107.
Harper, William M., xi.
Hartley, 130, 136, 181.
Harvey, Gabriel, 6, 7, 8, 15.
Hazlitt, xiv.
Henry VIII, 162.
Home, 93.
Homer, 19, 113, 117.
Horace, 8, 9, 11, 23, 28, 36, 112, 117, 129.
Hutchinson, Thomas, xi, 144.
Hutton, R. H., xi.

Jeffrey, 90.
Johnson, Samuel, 11, 23, 30, 31, 44, 54, 58, 60, 66, 123, 133.
Jonson, Ben, 13, 14, 16, 21, 22, 25.
Julleville, Petit de, 22, 26.

INDEX OF PROPER NAMES

Juvenal, 112.

Keats, 86, 105.
Kellner, 152, 156.
Klopstock, 123.
Knight, 78, 80.

LaBruyére, 55.
Lamb, vii, viii, x, xiv, 73, 113, 118, 119, 122, 123, 124, 125, 127, 128, 181.
Landon, xiv.
Langhorne, 94.
Legouis, xi, 64, 65, 76, 77, 83, 84, 93, 95, 98, 102, 109.
Lloyd, 125.
Longinus, 52, 129.
Lucretius, 62, 113.

Malherbe, 22, 23, 26, 27, 30, 33.
Matthews, 108, 112.
Milton, 4, 16-18, 19, 24, 32, 49, 58, 59, 60, 62, 63, 71, 87, 91, 92, 93, 96, 97, 98, 99, 100, 111, 114, 116, 117, 181, 182.

Nash, 8.

Ovid, 113, 117.

Parnell, 61.
Pater, 129.
Percy, 122, 123, 124.
Philips, Ambrose, 47.
Pléiade, 23.
Pope, 15, 22, 24, 26, 32-40, 49-57, 58, 60, 61, 73, 87, 88, 93, 114, 115, 118, 129.
Pratt, Alice, 105.
Prior, 40.
Puttenham, 10, 11, 20.

Quintilian, 9, 11.

Rogers, Samuel, 94.
Ronsard, 23.
Rosset, 93.

Seward, 118.
Scott, John, 57, 109.
Scott, Walter, xiv, 14, 42.
Shairp, xi.
Shakespeare, 4, 17, 19, 22, 32, 60, 71, 93, 99, 111, 114, 115, 116, 126, 150, 178.
Shelley, 129.
Sidney, Sir Philip, 7, 9, 10, 12, 14, 15, 21.
Skeat, 144.
Smollett, 93.
Sophocles, 19.
Southey, xiv, 118, 119, 120, 125.
Spence, 37.
Spenser, 2, 4, 5, 7, 8, 9, 10, 15, 17, 19, 58, 61, 71, 93, 99, 110, 111, 181.
Spinoza, 130.
Sprat, 27.
Steele, 52.
Swift, 39, 40, 51, 53.

Tasso, 111.
Taylor, William, 122, 123.
Tennyson, 182.
Terence, 9, 113.
Thelwell, 119, 122.
Theocritus, 103, 117.
Thomson, 55-57, 93, 99.

Virgil, 43, 53, 113, 117, 181.

Waller, 16, 23, 26, 34, 45, 47, 49.
Warton, Joseph, 38, 53, 55-57, 62, 85, 87, 92, 114.
Walsh, 33.
Watts, 46.
Wilson, 10.
Winchelsea, Lady, 88, 93.
Wolsely, Robert, 28.
Wordsworth, Christopher, 106, 107, 168.
Wordsworth, Dorothy, 106, 107.
Wrangham, 112.

Young, 93, 99.

YALE STUDIES IN ENGLISH.

Albert S. Cook, Editor.

I. The Foreign Sources of Modern English Versification. Charlton M. Lewis, Ph.D. $0.50.

II. Ælfric: A New Study of his Life and Writings. Caroline Louisa White, Ph.D. $1.50.

III. The Life of St. Cecelia, from MS. Ashmole 43 and MS. Cotton Tiberius E. VII, with Introduction, Variants, and Glossary. Bertha Ellen Lovewell, Ph.D. $1.00.

IV. Dryden's Dramatic Theory and Practice. Margaret Sherwood, Ph.D. $0.50.

V. Studies in Jonson's Comedy. Elisabeth Woodbridge, Ph.D. $0.50.

VI. A Glossary of the West Saxon Gospels, Latin-West Saxon and West Saxon-Latin. Mattie Anstice Harris, Ph.D. $1.50.

VII. Andreas: The Legend of St. Andrew, translated from the Old English, with an Introduction. Robert Kilburn Root, Ph.D. $0.50.

VIII. The Classical Mythology of Milton's English Poems. Charles Grosvenor Osgood, Ph.D. $1.00.

IX. A Guide to the Middle English Metrical Romances dealing with English and Germanic Legends, and with the Cycles of Charlemagne and of Arthur. Anna Hunt Billings, Ph.D. $1.50.

X. The Earliest Lives of Dante, translated from the Italian of Giovanni Boccaccio and Lionardo Bruni Aretino. James Robinson Smith. $0.75.

XI. A Study in Epic Development. Irene T. Myers, Ph.D. $1.00.

XII. The Short Story. Henry Seidel Canby, Ph.D. $0.30.

XIII. King Alfred's Old English Version of St. Augustine's Soliloquies, edited with Introduction, Notes, and Glossary. Henry Lee Hargrove, Ph.D. $1.00.

XIV. The Phonology of the Northumbrian Gloss of St. Matthew. Emily Howard Foley, Ph.D. $0.75.

XV. Essays on the Study and Use of Poetry by Plutarch and Basil the Great, translated from the Greek, with an Introduction. FREDERICK MORGAN PADELFORD, Ph.D. $0.75.

XVI. The Translations of Beowulf: A Critical Bibliography. CHAUNCEY B. TINKER, Ph.D. $0.75.

XVII. The Alchemist, by Ben Jonson, edited with Introduction, Notes, and Glossary. CHARLES M. HATHAWAY, JR., Ph.D. $2.50. Cloth, $3.00.

XVIII. The Expression of Purpose in Old English Prose. HUBERT GIBSON SHEARIN, Ph.D. $1.00.

XIX. Classical Mythology in Shakespeare. ROBERT KILBURN ROOT, Ph.D. $1.00.

XX. The Controversy between the Puritans and the Stage. ELBERT N. S. THOMPSON, Ph.D. $2.00.

XXI. The Elene of Cynewulf, translated into English Prose. LUCIUS HUDSON HOLT, Ph.D. $0.30.

XXII. King Alfred's Old English Version of St. Augustine's Soliloquies, turned into Modern English. HENRY LEE HARGROVE, Ph.D. $0.75.

XXIII. The Cross in the Life and Literature of the Anglo-Saxons. WILLIAM O. STEVENS, Ph.D. $0.75.

XXIV. An Index to the Old English Glosses of the Durham Hymnarium. HARVEY W. CHAPMAN. $0.75.

XXV. Bartholomew Fair, by Ben Jonson, edited with Introduction, Notes, and Glossary. CARROLL STORRS ALDEN, Ph.D. $2.00.

XXVI. Select Translations from Scaliger's Poetics. FREDERICK M. PADELFORD, Ph.D. $0.75.

XXVII. Poetaster, by Ben Jonson, edited with Introduction, Notes, and Glossary. HERBERT S. MALLORY, Ph.D. $2.00. Cloth, $2.50.

XXVIII. The Staple of News, by Ben Jonson, edited with Introduction, Notes, and Glossary. DE WINTER, Ph.D. $2.00. Cloth, $2.50.

XXIX. The Devil is an Ass, by Ben Jonson, edited with Introduction, Notes, and Glossary. WILLIAM SAVAGE JOHNSON, Ph.D. $2.00. Cloth, $2.50.

XXX. The Language of the Northumbrian Gloss to the Gospel of St. Luke. MARGARET DUTTON KELLUM, Ph.D. $0.75.

XXXI. Epicœne, or the Silent Woman, by Ben Jonson, edited with Introduction, Notes, and Glossary. AURELIA HENRY, Ph.D. $2.00. Cloth, $2.50.

XXXII. The Syntax of the Temporal Clause in Old English Prose. ARTHUR ADAMS, Ph.D. $1.00.

XXXIII. The Knight of the Burning Pestle, by Beaumont and Fletcher, edited with Introduction, Notes, and Glossary. HERBERT S. MURCH, Ph.D. $2.00.

XXXIV. The New Inn, by Ben Jonson, edited with Introduction, Notes, and Glossary. GEORGE BREMNER TENNANT, Ph.D. $2.00.

XXXV. A Glossary of Wulfstan's Homilies. LORING HOLMES DODD, Ph.D. $1.00.

XXXVI. The Complaint of Nature, translated from the Latin of Alain de Lille. DOUGLAS M. MOFFAT, M.A. $0.75.

XXXVII. The Collaboration of Webster and Dekker. FREDERICK ERASTUS PIERCE, Ph.D. $1.00.

XXXVIII. English Nativity Plays, edited with Introduction, Notes, and Glossary. SAMUEL B. HEMINGWAY, Ph.D. $2.00. Cloth, $2.50.

XXXIX. Concessive Constructions in Old English Prose. JOSEPHINE MAY BURNHAM, Ph.D. $1.00.

XL. The Tenure of Kings and Magistrates, by John Milton, edited with Introduction and Notes. WILLIAM TALBOT ALLISON, Ph.D. $1.25.

XLI. Biblical Quotations in Middle English Literature before 1350. MARY W. SMYTH, Ph.D. $2.00.

XLII. The Dialogue in English Literature. ELIZABETH MERRILL, Ph.D. $1.00.

XLIII. A Study of Tindale's Genesis, compared with the Genesis of Coverdale and of the Authorized Version. ELIZABETH WHITTLESEY CLEAVELAND, Ph.D. $2.00.

XLIV. The Presentation of Time in the Elizabethan Drama. MABLE BULAND, Ph.D. $1.50.

XLV. Cynthia's Revels, or the Fountain of Self-Love, by Ben Jonson, edited with Introduction, Notes, and Glossary. ALEXANDER CORBIN JUDSON, Ph.D. $2.00.

XLVI. Richard Brome: A Study of his Life and Works. CLARENCE EDWARD ANDREWS, Ph.D. $1.25.

XLVII. The Magnetic Lady, or Humors Reconciled, by Ben Jonson, edited with Introduction, Notes, and Glossary. HARVEY WHITEFIELD PECK, Ph.D. $2.00.

XLVIII. Genesis A (sometimes attributed to Cædmon) translation from the Old English. LAWRENCE MASON, Ph.D. $0.75.

XLIX. The Later Version of the Wycliffite Epistle to the Romans, compared with the Latin Original: A Study of Wycliffite English. EMMA CURTISS TUCKER, Ph.D. $1.50.

L. Some Accounts of the Bewcastle Cross between the Years 1607 and 1861. ALBERT STANBURROUGH COOK. $1.50.

LI. The Ready and Easy Way to Establish a Free Commonwealth, by John Milton, edited with Introduction, Notes, and Glossary. EVERT MORDECAI CLARK, Ph.D. $1.50.

LII. Every Man in his Humour, by Ben Jonson, edited with Introduction, Notes and Glossary. HENRY HOLLAND CARTER, Ph.D. $2.00.

LIII. Catiline, his Conspiracy, by Ben Jonson, edited with Introduction, Notes, and Glossary. LYNN HAROLD HARRIS, Ph.D. $2.00.

LIV. Of Reformation, touching Church-Discipline in England, by John Milton, edited with Introduction, Notes, and Glossary. WILL TALIAFERRO HALE, Ph.D. $2.00.

LV. Old English Scholarship in England from 1566 to 1800. ELEANOR N. ADAMS, Ph.D. $2.00.

LVI. The Case is Altered, by Ben Jonson, edited with Introduction, Notes, and Glossary. WILLIAM EDWARD SELIN, Ph.D. $2.00.

LVII. Wordsworth's Theory of Poetic Diction: A Study of the Historical and Personal Background of the Lyrical Ballads. MARJORIE LATTA BARSTOW. $1.50.

DATE DUE			
MAR 2~~0~~ 1967			
~~SEP 2 0 1967~~			
JAN 5 - 1967			
~~DEC~~ OCT 29 '73			
DEC 8 '76			
APR 15 1985			
FEB 01 1994			
GAYLORD			PRINTED IN U.S.A.